MOLIÈRE'S
TARTUFFE

COMEDY IN FIVE ACTS, 1669

TRANSLATED INTO ENGLISH VERSE
BY RICHARD WILBUR

★

★

DRAMATISTS
PLAY SERVICE
INC.

To my brother Lawrence

INTRODUCTION

There may be people who deny comedy the right to be serious, and think it improper for any but trivial themes to consort with laughter. It would take people of that kind to find in *Tartuffe* anything offensive to religion. The warped characters of the play express an obviously warped religious attitude, which is corrected by the reasonable orthodoxy of Cléante, the wholesomeness of Dorine, and the entire testimony of the action. The play is not a satire on religion, as those held who kept it off the boards for five years. Is it, then, a satire on religious hypocrisy, as Molière claimed in his polemical preface of 1669?

The play speaks often of religious hypocrisy, displays it in action, and sometimes seems to be gesturing toward its practioners in seventeenth-century French society. Tartuffe is made to recommend, more than once, those Jesuitical techniques for easing the conscience which Pascal attacked in the *Provincial Letters.* Cléante makes a long speech against people who feign piety for the sake of preferment or political advantage. And yet no one in the play can be said to be a religious hypocrite in any representative sense. Tartuffe may at times suggest or symbolize the slippery casuist, or the sort of hypocrite denounced by Cléante, but he is not himself such a person. He is a versatile parasite or confidence man, with a very long criminal record, and to pose as a holy man is not his only *modus operandi:* we see him, in the last act, shifting easily from the role of saint to that of hundred-percenter. As for the other major characters who might qualify, Madame Pernelle is simply a nasty bigot, while the religious attitudes of her son Orgon are, for all their underlying corruption, quite sincere.

Tartuffe is only incidentally satiric; what we experience in reading or seeing it, as several modern critics have argued, is not a satire but a "deep" comedy in which (1) a knave tries to control life by cold chicanery, (2) a fool tries to oppress life by unconscious misuse of the highest values, and (3) life, happily, will not have it.

Orgon, the central character of the play, is a rich bourgeois of

5

middle age, with two grown children by his first wife. His second wife, Elmire, is attractive, young, and socially clever. We gather from the maid Dorine that Orgon has until lately seemed a good and sensible man, but the Orgon whom we meet in Act I, Scene 4 has become a fool. What has happened to him? It appears that he, like many another middle-aged man, has been alarmed by a sense of failing powers and failing authority, and that he has compensated by adopting an extreme religious severity. In this he is comparable to the aging coquette described by Dorine, who "quits a world which fast is quitting her," and saves face by becoming a censorious prude.

Orgon's resort to bigotry has coincided with his discovery of Tartuffe, a wily opportunist who imposes upon him by a pretense of sanctity, and is soon established in Orgon's house as honored guest, spiritual guide, and moral censor. Tartuffe's attitude toward Orgon is perfectly simple: he regards his benefactor as a dupe, and proposes to swindle him as badly as he can. Orgon's attitude toward Tartuffe is more complex and far less conscious. It consists, in part, of an unnatural fondness or "crush" about which the clearsighted Dorine is explicit:

> *He pets and pampers him with love more tender*
> *Than any pretty mistress could engender . . . .*

It also involves, in the strict sense of the word, idolatry: Orgon's febrile religious emotions are all related to Tartuffe and appear to terminate in him. Finally, and least consciously, Orgon cherishes Tartuffe because, with the sanction of the latter's austere precepts, he can tyrannize over his family and punish them for possessing what he feels himself to be losing: youth, gaiety, strong natural desires. This punitive motive comes to the surface, looking like plain sadism, when Orgon orders his daughter to

> *Marry Tartuffe, and mortify your flesh!*

Orgon is thus both Tartuffe's victim and his unconscious exploiter;

6

once we apprehend this, we can better understand Orgon's stubborn refusal to see Tartuffe for the fraud that he is.

When Orgon says to Cléante,

> *My mother, children, brother and wife could die,*
> *And I'd not feel a single moment's pain,*

he is parodying or perverting a Christian idea which derives from the Gospels and rings out purely in Luther's "A Mighty Fortress is Our God":

> *Let goods and kindred go,*
> *This mortal life also . . . .*

The trouble with Orgon's high spirituality is that one cannot obey the first commandment without obeying the second also. Orgon has withdrawn all proper feeling from those about him, and his vicious fatuity creates an atmosphere which is the comic equivalent of *King Lear's*. All natural bonds of love and trust are strained or broken; evil is taken for good; truth must to kennel. Cléante's reasonings, the rebellious protests of Damis, the entreaties of Mariane, and the mockeries of Dorine are ineffectual against Orgon's folly; he must see Tartuffe paw at his wife, and hear Tartuffe speak contemptuously of him, before he is willing to part with the sponsor of his spiteful piety. How little "religion" there has been in Orgon's behavior, how much it has arisen from infatuation and bitterness, we may judge by his indiscriminate outburst in the fifth act:

> *Enough, by God! I'm through with pious men!*
> *Henceforth I'll hate the whole false brotherhood,*
> *And persecute them worse than Satan could.*

By the time Orgon is made to see Tartuffe's duplicity, the latter has accomplished his swindle, and is in a position to bring about Orgon's material ruin. It takes Louis XIV himself to save the day, in a conclusion which may seem both forced and flattering, but which serves to contrast a judicious, humane and forgiving ruler with the domestic tyrant Orgon. The King's moral insight is Tartuffe's final undoing; nevertheless there is an earlier scene in which we are given better assurance of the invincibility of the natural and sane. I refer to Tartuffe's first conversation with Elmire, in which passion compels the hypocrite recklessly to abandon his role. What comes out of Tartuffe in that scene is an expression of helpless lust, couched in an appalling mixture of the languages of gallantry and devotion. It is not attractive; and yet one is profoundly satisfied to discover that, as W.G. Moore puts it, "Tartuffe's human nature escapes his calculation." To be flawlessly monstrous is, thank heaven, not easy.

In translating *Tartuffe* I have tried, as with *The Misanthrope* some years ago, to reproduce with all possible fidelity both Molière's words and his poetic form. The necessity of keeping verse and rhyme, in such plays as these, was argued at some length in an introduction to the earlier translation, and I shall not repeat all those arguments here. It is true that *Tartuffe* presents an upper-bourgeois rather than a courtly milieu; there is less deliberate wit and elegance than in the dialogue of *The Misanthrope*, and consequently there is less call for the couplet as a conveyor of epigrammatic effects. Yet there are such effects in *Tartuffe*, and rhyme and verse are required here for other good reasons: to pay out the long speeches with clarifying emphasis, and at an assimilable rate; to couple farcical sequences to passages of greater weight and resonance; and to give a purely formal pleasure, as when balancing verse-patterns support the "Ballet" movement of the close of Act II. My convictions being what they are, I am happy to report what a number of productions of the *Misanthrope* translation have shown: that contemporary audiences are quite willing to put up with rhymed verse on the stage.

I thank Messrs. Jacques Barzun and Eric Bentley for encouraging me to undertake this translation; Messrs. Harry Levin, Frederic Musser and Edward Williamson for suggesting improvements in the text; and the Ford and Philadelphia Community Foundations for their support of the project.

Richard Wilbur

Portland, Connecticut
February, 1963

CHARACTERS

MME. PERNELLE, Orgon's mother

ORGON, Elmire's husband

ELMIRE, Orgon's wife

DAMIS, Orgon's son, Elmire's stepson

MARIANE, Orgon's daughter, Elmire's stepdaughter,
in love with Valère

VALÈRE, in love with Mariane

CLÉANTE, Orgon's brother-in-law

TARTUFFE, a hypocrite

DORINE, Mariane's lady's-maid

M. LOYAL, a baliff

A POLICE OFFICER

FLIPOTE, Mme Pernelle's maid

The scene throughout: Orgon's house in Paris

TARTUFFE

ACT I
SCENE ONE

MADAME PERNELLE and FLIPOTE, her maid,
ELMIRE, MARIANE, DORINE, DAMIS, CLÉANTE

MADAME PERNELLE.
Come. come, Flipote; it's time I left this place.
ELMIRE.
I can't keep up, you walk at such a pace.
MADAME PERNELLE.
Don't trouble, child; no need to show me out.
It's not your manners I'm concerned about.
ELMIRE.
We merely pay you the respect we owe.
But, Mother, why this hurry? Must you go?
MADAME PERNELLE.
I must. This house appals me. No one in it
Will pay attention for a single minute.
Children, I take my leave much vexed in spirit.
I offer good advice, but you won't hear it.
You all break in and chatter on and on.
It's like a madhouse with the keeper gone.
DORINE.
If ...
MADAME PERNELLE.
    Girl, you talk too much, and I'm afraid
You're far too saucy for a lady's-maid.
You push in everywhere and have your say.

DAMIS.

But...

MADAME PERNELLE.

      You, boy, grow more foolish every day.
To think my grandson should be such a dunce!
I've said a hundred times, if I've said it once,
That if you keep the course on which you've started,
You'll leave your worthy father broken-hearted.

MARIANE.

I think...

MADAME PERNELLE.

      And you, his sister, seem so pure,
So shy, so innocent, and so demure.
But you know what they say about still waters.
I pity parents with secretive daughters.

ELMIRE.

Now, Mother...

MADAME PERNELLE.

      And as for you, child, let me add
That your behavior is extremely bad,
And a poor example for these children, too.
Their dear, dead mother did far better than you.
You're much too free with money, and I'm distressed
To see you so elaborately dressed.
When it's one's husband that one aims to please,
One has no need of costly fripperies.

CLÉANTE.

Oh, Madam, really...

MADAME PERNELLE.

      You are her brother, Sir,
And I respect and love you; yet if I were
My son, this lady's good and pious spouse,
I wouldn't make you welcome in my house.
You're full of worldly counsels which, I fear,
Aren't suitable for decent folk to hear.
I've spoken bluntly, Sir; but it behooves us
Not to mince words when righteous fervor moves us.

DAMIS.
Your man Tartuffe is full of holy speeches...
MADAME PERNELLE.
And practises precisely what he preaches.
He's a fine man, and should be listened to.
I will not hear him mocked by fools like you.
DAMIS.
Good God! Do you expect me to submit
To the tyranny of that carping hypocrite?
Must we forgo all joys and satisfactions
Because that bigot censures all our actions?
DORINE.
To hear him talk—and he talks all the time—
There's nothing one can do that's not a crime.
He rails at everything, your dear Tartuffe.
MADAME PERNELLE.
Whatever he reproves deserves reproof.
He's out to save your souls, and all of you
Must love him, as my son would have you do.
DAMIS.
Ah no, Grandmother, I could never take
To such a rascal, even for my father's sake.
That's how I feel, and I shall not dissemble.
His every action makes me seethe and tremble
With helpless anger, and I have no doubt
That he and I will shortly have it out.
DORINE.
Surely it is a shame and a disgrace
To see this man usurp the master's place—
To see this beggar who, when first he came,
Had not a shoe or shoestring to his name
So far forget himself that he behaves
As if the house were his, and we his slaves.
MADAME PERNELLE.
Well, mark my words, your souls would fare far better
If you obeyed his precepts to the letter.

DORINE.
You see him as a saint. I'm far less awed;
In fact, I see right through him. He's a fraud.
MADAME PERNELLE.
Nonsense!
DORINE.
        His man Laurent's the same, or worse;
I'd not trust either with a penny purse.
MADAME PERNELLE.
I can't say what his servant's morals may be;
His own great goodness I can guarantee.
You all regard him with distaste and fear
Because he tells you what you're loath to hear,
Condemns your sins, points out your moral flaws,
And humbly strives to further Heaven's cause.
DORINE.
If sin is all that bothers him, why is it
He's so upset when folk drop in to visit?
Is Heaven so outraged by a social call
That he must prophesy against us all?
I'll tell you what I think: if you ask me,
He's jealous of my mistress' company.
MADAME PERNELLE.
Rubbish!
(To Elmire:)
      He's not alone, child, in complaining
Of all of your promiscuous entertaining.
Why, the whole neighborhood's upset, I know,
By all these carriages that come and go,
With crowds of guests parading in and out
And noisy servants loitering about.
In all of this, I'm sure there's nothing vicious;
But why give people cause to be suspicious?
CLÉANTE.
They need no cause; they'll talk in any case.
Madam, this world would be a joyless place

If, fearing what malicious tongues might say,
We locked our doors and turned our friends away.
And even if one did so dreary a thing,
D'you think those tongues would cease their chattering?
One can't fight slander; it's a losing battle;
Let us instead ignore their tittle-tattle.
Let's strive to live by conscience' clear decrees,
And let the gossips gossip as they please.
DORINE.
If there is talk against us, I know the source:
It's Daphne and her little husband, of course.
Those who have greatest cause for guilt and shame
Are quickest to besmirch a neighbor's name.
When there's a chance for libel, they never miss it;
When something can be made to seem illicit
They're off at once to spread the joyous news,
Adding to fact what fantasies they choose.
By talking up their neighbor's indiscretions
They seek to camouflage their own transgressions,
Hoping that others' innocent affairs
Will lend a hue of innocence to theirs,
Or that their own black guilt will come to seem
Part of a general shady color-scheme.
MADAME PERNELLE.
All that is quite irrelevant. I doubt
That anyone's more virtuous and devout
Than dear Orante; and I'm informed that she
Condemns your mode of life most vehemently.
DORINE.
Oh, yes, she's strict, devout, and has no taint
Of worldliness; in short, she seems a saint.
But it was time which taught her that disguise;
She's thus because she can't be otherwise.
So long as her attractions could enthrall,
She flounced and flirted and enjoyed it all,
But now that they're no longer what they were

15

She quits a world which fast is quitting her,
And wears a veil of virtue of conceal
Her bankrupt beauty and her lost appeal.
That's what becomes of old coquettes today:
Distressed when all their lovers fall away,
They see no recourse but to play the prude,
And so confer a style on solitude.
Thereafter, they're severe with everyone,
Condemning all our actions, pardoning none,
And claiming to be pure, austere, and zealous
When, if the truth were known, they're merely jealous,
And cannot bear to see another know
The pleasures time has forced them to forgo.
MADAME PERNELLE.   *(Initially to Elmire.)*
That sort of talk is what you like to hear;
Therefore you'd have us all keep still, my dear,
While Madam rattles on the livelong day.
Nevertheless, I mean to have my say.
I tell you that you're blest to have Tartuffe
Dwelling, as my son's guest, beneath this roof;
That Heaven has sent him to forestall its wrath
By leading you, once more, to the true path;
That all he reprehends is reprehensible,
And that you'd better heed him, and be sensible.
These visits, balls, and parties in which you revel
Are nothing but inventions of the Devil.
One never hears a word that's edifying:
Nothing but chaff and foolishness and lying,
As well as vicious gossip in which one's neighbor
Is cut to bits with epee, foil, and saber.
People of sense are driven half-insane
At such affairs, where noise and folly reign
And reputations perish thick and fast.
As a wise preacher said on Sunday last,
Parties are Towers of Babylon, because
The guests all babble on with never a pause;

And then he told a story which, I think...
(To Cléante.)
I heard that laugh, Sir, and I saw that wink!
Go find your silly friends and laugh some more!
Enough; I'm going; don't show me to the door.
I leave this household much dismayed and vexed;
I cannot say when I shall see you next.
(Slapping Flipote.)
Wake up, don't stand there gaping into space!
I'll slap some sense into that stupid face.
Move, move, you slut.

SCENE TWO

CLÉANTE, DORINE

CLÉANTE.

               I think I'll stay behind;
I want no further pieces of her mind.
How that old lady...
DORINE.

              Oh, what wouldn't she say
If she could hear you speak of her that way!
She'd thank you for the *lady*, but I'm sure
She'd find the *old* a little premature.
CLÉANTE.
My, what a scene she made, and what a din!
And how this man Tartuffe has taken her in!
DORINE.
Yes, but her son is even worse deceived;
His folly must be seen to be believed.
In the late troubles, he played an able part
And served his king with wise and loyal heart,

But he's quite lost his senses since he fell
Beneath Tartuffe's infatuating spell.
He calls him brother, and loves him as his life,
Preferring him to mother, child, or wife.
In him and him alone will he confide;
He's made him his confessor and his guide;
He pets and pampers him with love more tender
Than any pretty mistress could engender,
Gives him the place of honor when they dine,
Delights to see him gorging like a swine,
Stuffs him with dainties till his guts distend,
And when he belches, cries "God bless you, friend!"
In short, he's mad; he worships him; he dotes;
His deeds he marvels at, his words he quotes,
Thinking each act a miracle, each word
Oracular as those that Moses heard.
Tartuffe, much pleased to find so easy a victim,
Has in a hundred ways beguiled and tricked him,
Milked him of money, and with his permission
Established here a sort of Inquisition.
Even Laurent, his lackey, dares to give
Us arrogant advice on how to live;
He sermonizes us in thundering tones
And confiscates our ribbons and colognes.
Last week he tore a kerchief into pieces
Because he found it pressed in a *Life of Jesus:*
He said it was a sin to juxtapose
Unholy vanities and holy prose.

SCENE THREE

ELMIRE. *(To Cléante.)*
You did well not to follow; she stood in the door
And said *verbatim* all she'd said before.
I saw my husband coming. I think I'd best
Go upstairs now, and take a little rest.
CLÉANTE.
I'll wait and greet him here; then I must go.
I've really only time to say hello.
DAMIS.
Sound him about my sister's wedding, please.
I think Tartuffe's against it, and that he's
Been urging Father to withdraw his blessing.
As you well know, I'd find that most distressing.
Unless my sister and Valère can marry,
My hopes to wed *his* sister will miscarry,
And I'm determined...
DORINE.

He's coming.

SCENE FOUR

ORGON.

Ah, Brother, good-day.

CLÉANTE.
Well, welcome back. I'm sorry I can't stay.
How was the country? Blooming, I trust, and green?
ORGON.
Excuse me, Brother; just one moment.
(To Dorine.)

                                        Dorine...

(To Cléante.)
To put my mind at rest, I always learn
The household news the moment I return.
(To Dorine.)
Has all been well, these two days I've been gone?
How are the family? What's been going on?
DORINE.
Your wife, two days ago, had a bad fever,
And a fierce headache which refused to leave her.
ORGON.
Ah. And Tartuffe?
DORINE.

                    Tartuffe? Why, he's round and red,
Bursting with health, and excellently fed.
ORGON.
Poor fellow!
DORINE.

                    That night, the mistress was unable
To take a single bite at the dinner-table.
Her headache-pains, she said, were simply hellish.
ORGON.
Ah. And Tartuffe?
DORINE.

                    He ate his meal with relish,
And zealously devoured in her presence
A leg of mutton and a brace of pheasants.
ORGON.
Poor fellow!
DORINE.

                    Well, the pains continued strong,

20

And so she tossed and tossed the whole night long,
Now icy-cold, now burning like a flame.
We sat beside her bed till morning came.
ORGON.
Ah. And Tartuffe?
DORINE.

           Why, having eaten, he rose
And sought his room, already in a doze,
Got into his warm bed, and snored away
In perfect peace until the break of day.
ORGON.
Poor fellow!
DORINE.

         After much ado, we talked her
Into dispatching someone for the doctor.
He bled her, and the fever quickly fell.
ORGON.
Ah. And Tartuffe?
DORINE.

         He bore it very well.
To keep his cheerfulness at any cost,
And make up for the blood *Madame* had lost,
He drank, at lunch, four beakers full of port.
ORGON.
Poor fellow!
DORINE.

       Both are doing well, in short.
I'll go and tell *Madame* that you've expressed
Keen sympathy and anxious interest.

SCENE FIVE

ORGON, CLÉANTE

CLÉANTE.
That girl was laughing in your face, and though
I've no wish to offend you, even so
I'm bound to say that she had some excuse.
How can you possibly be such a goose?
Are you so dazed by this man's hocus-pocus
That all the world, save him, is out of focus?
You've given him clothing, shelter, food, and care;
Why must you also...
ORGON.
      Brother, stop right there.
You do not know the man of whom you speak.
CLÉANTE.
I grant you that. But my judgement's not so weak
That I can't tell, by his effect on others...
ORGON.
Ah, when you meet him, you two will be like brothers!
There's been no loftier soul since time began.
He is a man who...a man who...an excellent man.
To keep his precepts is to be reborn,
And view this dunghill of a world with scorn.
Yes, thanks to him I'm a changed man indeed.
Under his tutelage my soul's been freed
From earthly loves, and every human tie:
My mother, children, brother, and wife could die,
And I'd not feel a single moment's pain.

CLÉANTE.

That's a fine sentiment, Brother; most humane.

ORGON.

Oh, had you seen Tartuffe as I first knew him,
Your heart, like mine, would have surrendered to him.
He used to come into our church each day
And humbly kneel nearby, and start to pray.
He'd draw the eyes of everybody there
By the deep fervor of his heartfelt prayer;
He'd sigh and weep, and sometimes with a sound
Of rapture he would bend and kiss the ground;
And when I rose to go, he'd run before
To offer me holy-water at the door.
His serving-man, no less devout than he,
Informed me of his master's poverty;
I gave him gifts, but in his humbleness
He'd beg me every time to give him less.
"Oh, that's too much," he'd cry, "too much by twice!
I don't deserve it. The half, Sir, would suffice."
And when I wouldn't take it back, he'd share
Half of it with the poor, right then and there.
At length, Heaven prompted me to take him in
To dwell with us, and free our souls from sin.
He guides our lives, and to protect my honor
Stays by my wife, and keeps an eye upon her;
He tells me whom she sees, and all she does,
And seems more jealous than I ever was!
And how austere he is! Why, he can detect
A mortal sin where you would least suspect;
In smallest trifles, he's extremely strict.
Last week, his conscience was severely pricked
Because, while praying, he had caught a flea
And killed it, so he felt, too wrathfully.

CLÉANTE.

Good God, man! Have you lost your common sense—
Or is this all some joke at my expense?
How can you stand there and in all sobriety...

ORGON.
Brother, your language savors of impiety.
Too much free-thinking's made your faith unsteady,
And as I've warned you many times already,
'Twill get you into trouble before you're through.
CLÉANTE.
So, I've been told before by dupes like you:
Being blind, you'd have all others blind as well;
The clear-eyed man you call an infidel,
And he who sees through humbug and pretense
Is charged, by you, with want of reverence.
Spare me your warnings, Brother; I have no fear
Of speaking out, for you and Heaven to hear,
Against affected zeal and pious knavery.
There's true and false in piety, as in bravery,
And just as those whose courage shines the most
In battle, are the least inclined to boast,
So those whose hearts are truly pure and lowly
Don't make a flashy show of being holy.
There's a vast difference, so it seems to me,
Between true piety and hypocrisy:
How do you fail to see it, may I ask?
Is not a face quite different from a mask?
Cannot sincerity and cunning art,
Reality and semblance, be told apart?
Are scarecrows just like men, and do you hold
That a false coin is just as good as gold?
Ah, Brother, man's a strangely fashioned creature
Who seldom is content to follow Nature,
But recklessly pursues his inclination
Beyond the narrow bounds of moderation,
And often, by transgressing Reason's laws,
Perverts a lofty aim or noble cause.
A passing observation, but it applies.
ORGON.
I see, dear Brother, that you're profoundly wise;

You harbor all the insight of the age.
You are our one clear mind, our only sage,
The era's oracle, its Cato too,
And all mankind are fools compared to you.
CLÉANTE.
Brother, I don't pretend to be a sage,
Nor have I all the wisdom of the age.
There's just one insight I would dare to claim:
I know that true and false are not the same;
And just as there is nothing I more revere
Than a soul whose faith is steadfast and sincere,
Nothing that I more cherish and admire
Than honest zeal and true religious fire,
So there is nothing that I find more base
Than specious piety's dishonest face—
Than these bold mountebanks, these histrios
Whose impious mummeries and hollow shows
Exploit our love of Heaven, and make a jest
Of all that men think holiest and best;
These calculating souls who offer prayers
Not to their Maker, but as public wares,
And seek to buy respect and reputation
With lifted eyes and sighs of exaltation;
These charlatans, I say, whose pilgrim souls
Proceed, by way of Heaven, toward earthly goals,
Who weep and pray and swindle and extort,
Who preach the monkish life, but haunt the court,
Who make their zeal the partner of their vice—
Such men are vengeful, sly, and cold as ice,
And when there is an enemy to defame
They cloak their spite in fair religion's name,
Their private spleen and malice being made
To seem a high and virtuous crusade,
Until, to mankind's reverent applause,
They crucify their foe in Heaven's cause.
Such knaves are all too common; yet, for the wise,

True piety isn't hard to recognize,
And, happily, these present times provide us
With bright examples to instruct and guide us.
Consider Ariston and Périandre;
Look at Oronte, Alcidamas, Clitandre;
Their virtue is ackowledged; who could doubt it?
But you won't hear them beat the drum about it.
They're never ostentatious, never vain,
And their religion's moderate and humane;
It's not their way to criticize and chide:
They think censoriousness a mark of pride,
And therefore, letting others preach and rave,
They show, by deeds, how Christians should behave.
They think no evil of their fellow man,
But judge of him as kindly as they can.
They don't intrigue and wangle and conspire;
To lead a good life is their one desire;
The sinner wakes no rancorous hate in them;
It is the sin alone which they condemn;
Nor do they try to show a fiercer zeal
For Heaven's cause than Heaven itself could feel.
These men I honor, these men I advocate
As models for us all to emulate.
Your man is not their sort at all, I fear:
And, while your praise of him is quite sincere,
I think that you've been dreadfully deluded.

ORGON.

Now then, dear Brother, is your speech concluded?

CLÉANTE.

Why, yes.

ORGON.

        Your servant, Sir.

(He turns to go.)

CLÉANTE.

                No, Brother; wait.

There's one more matter. You agreed of late
That young Valère might have your daughter's hand.

ORGON.
I did.
CLÉANTE.

      And set the date, I understand.
ORGON.
Quite so.
CLÉANTE.

        You've now postponed it; is that true?
ORGON.
No doubt.
CLÉANTE.

       The match no longer pleases you?
ORGON.
Who knows?
CLÉANTE.

        D'you mean to go back on your word?
ORGON.
I won't say that.
CLÉANTE.

         Has anything occurred
Which might entitle you to break your pledge?
ORGON.
Perhaps.
CLÉANTE.

      Why must you hem, and haw, and hedge?
The boy asked me to sound you in this affair...
ORGON.
It's been a pleasure.
CLÉANTE.

        But what shall I tell Valère?
ORGON.
Whatever you like.
CLÉANTE.

       But what have you decided?
What are your plans?

ORGON.

                    I plan, Sir, to be guided

By Heaven's will.

CLÉANTE.

                      Come, Brother, don't talk rot.

You've given Valère your word; will you keep it, or not?

ORGON.

Good day.

CLÉANTE.

                This looks like poor Valère's undoing;

I'll go and warn him that there's trouble brewing.

ACT II
SCENE ONE

ORGON, MARIANE

ORGON.
Mariane.
MARIANE.
      Yes, Father?
ORGON.
             A word with you; come here.
MARIANE.
What are you looking for?
ORGON. *(Peering into a small closet.)*
             Eavesdroppers, dear.
I'm making sure we shan't be overheard.
Someone in there could catch our every word.
Ah, good, we're safe. Now, Mariane, my child,
You're a sweet girl who's tractable and mild,
Whom I hold dear, and think most highly of.
MARIANE.
I'm deeply grateful, Father, for your love.
ORGON.
That's well said, Daughter; and you can repay me
If, in all things, you'll cheerfully obey me.
MARIANE.
To please you, Sir, is what delights me best.
ORGON.
Good, good. Now, what d'you think of Tartuffe, our guest?

MARIANE.

I, Sir?

ORGON.

      Yes. Weigh your answer; think it through.

MARIANE.

Oh, dear. I'll say whatever you wish me to.

ORGON.

That's wisely said, my Daughter. Say of him, then,
That he's the very worthiest of men,
And that you're fond of him, and would rejoice
In being his wife, if that should be my choice.
Well?

MARIANE.

    What?

ORGON.

      What's that?

MARIANE.

             I...

ORGON.

                  Well?

MARIANE.

                         Forgive me, pray.

ORGON.

Did you not hear me?

MARIANE.

                Of *whom*, Sir, must I say
That I am fond of him, and would rejoice
In being his wife, if that should be your choice?

ORGON.

Why, of Tartuffe.

MARIANE.

          But, Father, that's false, you know.
Why would you have me say what isn't so?

ORGON.

Because I am resolved it shall be true.
That it's my wish should be enough for you.

MARIANE.
You can't mean, Father...
ORGON.

Yes, Tartuffe shall be
Allied by marriage to this family,
And he's to be your husband, is that clear?
It's a father's privilege...

SCENE TWO

DORINE, ORGON, MARIANE

ORGON. *(To Dorine.)*

What are you doing in here?
Is curiosity so fierce a passion
With you, that you must eavesdrop in this fashion?
DORINE.
There's lately been a rumor going about—
Based on some hunch or chance remark, no doubt—
That you mean Mariane to wed Tartuffe.
I've laughed it off, of course, as just a spoof.
ORGON.
You find it so incredible?
DORINE.

Yes, I do.
I won't accept that story, even from you.
ORGON.
Well, you'll believe it when the thing is done.
DORINE.
Yes, yes, of course. Go on and have your fun.
ORGON.
I've never been more serious in my life.

DORINE.
Ha!
ORGON.

   Daughter, I mean it; you're to be his wife.

DORINE.
No, don't believe your father; it's all a hoax.
ORGON.
See here, young woman...
DORINE.

       Come, Sir, no more jokes;

You can't fool us.
ORGON.

     How dare you talk that way?

DORINE.
All right, then; we believe you, sad to say.
But how a man like you, who looks to wise
And wears a moustache of such splendid size,
Can be so foolish as to...
ORGON.

      Silence, please!

My girl, you take too many liberties.
I'm master here, as you must not forget.
DORINE.
Do let's discuss this calmly; don't be upset.
You can't be serious, Sir, about this plan.
What should that bigot want with Mariane?
Praying and fasting ought to keep him busy.
And then in terms of wealth and rank, what is he?
Why should a man of property like you
Pick out a beggar son-in-law?
ORGON.

       That will do.

Speak of his poverty with reverence.
His is a pure and saintly indigence
Which far transcends all worldly pride and pelf.
He lost his fortune, as he says himself,

32

Because he cared for Heaven alone, and so
Was careless of his interests here below.
I mean to get him out of his present straits
And help him to recover his estates—
Which, in his part of the world, have no small fame.
Poor though he is, he's a gentleman just the same.
DORINE.
Yes, so he tells us; and, Sir, it seems to me
Such pride goes very ill with piety.
A man whose spirit spurns this dungy earth
Ought not to brag of lands and noble birth;
Such worldly arrogance will hardly square
With meek devotion and the life of prayer.
...But this approach, I see, has drawn a blank;
Let's speak, then, of his person, not his rank.
Doesn't it seem to you a trifle grim
To give a girl like her to a man like him?
When two are so ill-suited, can't you see
What the sad consequence is bound to be?
A young girl's virtue is imperilled, Sir,
When such a marriage is imposed on her;
For if one's bridegroom isn't to one's taste,
It's hardly an inducement to be chaste,
And many a man with horns upon his brow
Has made his wife the thing that she is now.
It's hard to be a faithful wife, in short,
To certain husbands of a certain sort,
And he who gives his daughter to a man she hates
Must answer for her sins at Heaven's gates.
Think, Sir, before you play so risky a role.
ORGON.
This servant-girl presumes to save my soul!
DORINE.
You would do well to ponder what I've said.
ORGON.
Daughter, we'll disregard this dunderhead.

33

Just trust your father's judgement. Oh, I'm aware
That I once promised you to young Valère;
But now I hear he gambles, which greatly shocks me.
What's more, I've doubts about his orthodoxy.
His visits to church, I note, are very few.

DORINE.

Would you have him go at the same hours as you,
And kneel nearby, to be sure of being seen?

ORGON.

I can dispense with such remarks, Dorine.

(To Mariane.)

Tartuffe, however, is sure of Heaven's blessing,
And that's the only treasure worth possessing.
This match will bring you joys beyond all measure;
Your cup will overflow with every pleasure;
You two will interchange your faithful loves
Like two sweet cherubs, or two turtle-doves.
No harsh word shall be heard, no frown be seen,
And he shall make you happy as a queen.

DORINE.

And she'll make him a cuckold, just wait and see.

ORGON.

What language!

DORINE.

        Oh, he's a man of destiny;
He's *made* for horns, and what the stars demand
Your daughter's virtue surely can't withstand.

ORGON.

Don't interrupt me further. Why can't you learn
That certain things are none of your concern?

DORINE.

It's for your own sake that I interfere.

(She repeatedly interrupts Orgon just as he is turning to speak to his daughter.)

ORGON.

Most kind of you. Now, hold your tongue, d'you hear?

DORINE.
If I didn't love you...
ORGON.

Spare me your affection.

DORINE.
I'll love you, Sir, in spite of your objection.
ORGON.
Blast!
DORINE.

I can't bear, Sir, for your honor's sake,
To let you make this ludicrous mistake.
ORGON.
You mean to go on talking?
DORINE.

If I didn't protest
This sinful marriage, my conscience couldn't rest.
ORGON.
If you don't hold your tongue, you little shrew...
DORINE.
What, lost your temper? A pious man like you?
ORGON.
Yes! Yes! You talk and talk. I'm maddened by it.
Once and for all, I tell you to be quiet.
DORINE.
Well, I'll be quiet. But I'll be thinking hard.
ORGON.
Think all you like, but you had better guard
That saucy tongue of yours, or I'll...
(Turning back to Mariane.)

Now, child,

I've weighed this matter fully.
DORINE. *(Aside.)*

It drives me wild
That I can't speak.
(Orgon turns his head, and she is silent.)

ORGON.

Tartuffe is no young dandy,

But, still, his person...
DORINE. *(Aside.)*

Is as sweet as candy.

ORGON.
Is such that, even if you shouldn't care
For his other merits...
(He turns and stands facing Dorine, arms crossed.)
DORINE. *(Aside.)*

They'll make a lovely pair.

If I were she, no man would marry me
Against my inclination, and go scot-free.
He'd learn, before the wedding-day was over,
How readily a wife can find a lover.
ORGON.
(To Dorine.)
It seems you treat my orders as a joke.
DORINE.
Why, what's the matter? 'Twas not to you I spoke.
ORGON.
What *were* you doing?
DORINE.

Talking to myself, that's all.

ORGON.
Ah!
(Aside.)
One more bit of impudence and gall,
And I shall give her a good slap in the face.
(He puts himself in position to slap her; Dorine, whenever he glances at her, stands immobile and silent.)
Daughter, you shall accept, and with good grace,
The husband I've selected...Your wedding-day...
(To Dorine.)
Why don't you talk to yourself?
DORINE.

I've nothing to say.

36

ORGON.
Come, just one word.
DORINE.

           No thank you, Sir. I pass.
ORGON.
Come, speak; I'm waiting.
DORINE.

               I'd not be such an ass.
ORGON. *(Turning to Mariane.)*
In short, dear Daughter, I mean to be obeyed,
And you must bow to the sound choice I've made.
DORINE. *(Moving away.)*
I'd not wed such a monster, even in jest.
(Orgon attempts to slap her, but misses.)
ORGON.
Daughter, that maid of yours is a thorough pest;
She makes me sinfully annoyed and nettled.
I can't speak further; my nerves are too unsettled.
She's so upset me by her insolent talk,
I'll calm myself by going for a walk.

SCENE THREE

DORINE, MARIANE

DORINE. *(Returning.)*
Well, have you lost your tongue, girl? Must I play
Your part, and say the lines you ought to say?
Faced with a fate so hideous and absurd,
Can you not utter one dissenting word?
MARIANE.
What good would it do? A father's power is great.
DORINE.
Resist him now, or it will be too late.

MARIANE.

But...

DORINE.

   Tell him one cannot love at a father's whim;

That you shall marry for yourself, not him;

That since it's you who are to be the bride,

It's you, not he, who must be satisfied;

And that if his Tartuffe is so sublime,

He's free to marry him at any time.

MARIANE.

I've bowed so long to Father's strict control,

I couldn't oppose him now, to save my soul.

DORINE.

Come, come, Mariane. Do listen to reason, won't you?

Valere has asked your hand. Do you love him, or don't you?

MARIANE.

Oh, how unjust of you! What can you mean

By asking such a question, dear Dorine?

You know the depth of my affection for him;

I've told you a hundred times how I adore him.

DORINE.

I don't believe in everything I hear;

Who knows if your professions were sincere?

MARIANE.

They were, Dorine, and you do me wrong to doubt it;

Heaven knows that I've been all too frank about it.

DORINE.

You love him, then?

MARIANE.

     Oh, more than I can express.

DORINE.

And he, I take it, cares for you no less?

MARIANE.

I think so.

DORINE.

   And you both, with equal fire,

Burn to be married?

MARIANE.

That is our one desire.

DORINE.

What of Tartuffe, then? What of your father's plan?

MARIANE.

I'll kill myself, if I'm forced to wed that man.

DORINE.

I hadn't thought of that recourse. How splendid!
Just die, and all your troubles will be ended!
A fine solution. Oh, it maddens me
To hear you talk in that self-pitying key.

MARIANE.

Dorine, how harsh you are! It's most unfair.
You have no sympathy for my despair.

DORINE.

I've none at all for people who talk drivel
And, faced with difficulties, whine and snivel.

MARIANE.

No doubt I'm timid, but it would be wrong...

DORINE.

True love requires a heart that's firm and strong.

MARIANE.

I'm strong in my affection for Valère,
But coping with my father is his affair.

DORINE.

But if your father's brain has grown so cracked
Over his dear Tartuffe that he can retract
His blessing, though your wedding-day was named,
It's surely not Valère who's to be blamed.

MARIANE.

If I defied my father, as you suggest,
Would it not seem unmaidenly, at best?
Shall I defend my love at the expense
Of brazenness and disobedience?
Shall I parade my heart's desires, and flaunt...

DORINE.

No, I ask nothing of you. Clearly you want
To be Madame Tartuffe, and I feel bound
Not to oppose a wish so very sound.
What right have I to criticize the match?
Indeed, my dear, the man's a brilliant catch.
Monsieur Tartuffe! Now, there's a man of weight!
Yes, yes, Monsieur Tartuffe, I'm bound to state,
Is quite a person; that's not to be denied;
'Twill be no little thing to be his bride.
The world already rings with his renown;
He's a great noble—in his native town;
His ears are red, he has a pink complexion,
And all in all, he'll suit you to perfection.

MARIANE.

Dear God!

DORINE.

       Oh, how triumphant you will feel
At having caught a husband so ideal!

MARIANE.

Oh, do stop teasing, and use your cleverness
To get me out of this appalling mess.
Advise me, and I'll do whatever you say.

DORINE.

Ah no, a dutiful daughter must obey
Her father, even if he weds her to an ape.
You've a bright future; why struggle to escape?
Tartuffe will take you back where his family lives,
To a small town aswarm with relatives—
Uncles and cousins whom you'll be charmed to meet.
You'll be received at once by the elite,
Calling upon the bailiff's wife, no less—
Even, perhaps, upon the mayoress,
Who'll sit you down in the *best* kitchen chair.
Then, once a year, you'll dance at the village fair

To the drone of bagpipes—two of them, in fact—
And see a puppet-show, or an animal act.
Your husband...

MARIANE.

Oh, you turn my blood to ice!
Stop torturing me, and give me your advice.

DORINE. *(Threatening to go.)*
Your servant, Madam.

MARIANE.

Dorine, I beg of you...

DORINE.
No, you deserve it; this marriage must go through.

MARIANE.
Dorine!

DORINE.

No.

MARIANE.

Not Tartuffe! You know I think him...

DORINE.
Tartuffe's your cup of tea, and you shall drink him.

MARIANE.
I've always told you everything, and relied...

DORINE.
No. You deserve to be tartuffified.

MARIANE.
Well, since you mock me and refuse to care,
I'll henceforth seek my solace in despair:
Despair shall be my counsellor and friend,
And help me bring my sorrows to an end.
(She starts to leave.)

DORINE.
There now, come back; my anger has subsided.
You do deserve some pity, I've decided.

MARIANE.
Dorine, if Father makes me undergo
This dreadful martyrdom, I'll die, I know.

DORINE.
Don't fret; it won't be difficult to discover
Some plan of action...But here's Valère, your lover.

SCENE FOUR

VALÈRE, MARIANE, DORINE

VALÈRE.
Madam, I've just received some wondrous news
Regarding which I'd like to hear your views.
MARIANE.
What news?
VALÈRE.
    You're marrying Tartuffe.
MARIANE.
            I find
That Father does have such a match in mind.
VALÈRE.
Your father, Madam...
MARIANE.
       ...has just this minute said
That it's Tartuffe he wishes me to wed.
VALÈRE.
Can he be serious?
MARIANE.
      Oh, indeed he can;
He's clearly set his heart upon the plan.
VALÈRE.
And what position do you propose to take,
Madam?
MARIANE.
   Why—I don't know.

VALÈRE.

                    For heaven's sake—
You don't know?
MARIANE.

          No.

VALÈRE.

            Well, well!

MARIANE.

                    Advise me, do.

VALÈRE.
Marry the man. That's my advice to you.
MARIANE.
That's your advice?
VALÈRE.

          Yes.

MARIANE.

          Truly?

VALÈRE.

                    Oh, absolutely.
You couldn't choose more wisely, more astutely.
MARIANE.
Thanks for this counsel; I'll follow it, of course.
VALÈRE.
Do, do; I'm sure 'twill cost you no remorse.
MARIANE.
To give it didn't cause your heart to break.
VALÈRE.
I gave it, Madam, only for your sake.
MARIANE.
And it's for your sake that I take it, Sir.
DORINE. *(Withdrawing to the rear of the stage.)*
Let's see which fool will prove the stubborner.
VALÈRE.
So! I am nothing to you, and it was flat
Deception when you...

43

MARIANE.

                       Please, enough of that.
You've told me plainly that I should agree
To wed the man my father's chosen for me,
And since you've deigned to counsel me so wisely,
I promise, Sir, to do as you advise me.

VALÈRE.
Ah, no, 'twas not by me that you were swayed.
No, your decision was already made;
Though now, to save appearances, you protest
That you're betraying me at my behest.

MARIANE.
Just as you say.

VALÈRE.

                    Quite so. And I now see
That you were never truly in love with me.

MARIANE.
Alas, you're free to think so if you choose.

VALÈRE.
I choose to think so, and here's a bit of news:
You've spurned my hand, but I know where to turn
For kinder treatment, as you shall quickly learn.

MARIANE.
I'm sure you do. Your noble qualities
Inspire affection...

VALÈRE.

                  Forget my qualities, please.
They don't inspire you overmuch, I find.
But there's another lady I have in mind
Whose sweet and generous nature will not scorn
To compensate me for the loss I've borne.

MARIANE.
I'm no great loss, and I'm sure that you'll transfer
Your heart quite painlessly from me to her.

VALÈRE.
I'll do my best to take it in my stride.

The pain I feel at being cast aside
Time and forgetfulness may put an end to.
Or if I can't forget, I shall pretend to.
No self-respecting person is expected
To go on loving once he's been rejected.
MARIANE.
Now, that's a fine, high-minded sentiment.
VALÈRE.
One to which any sane man would assent.
Would you prefer it if I pined away
In hopeless passion till my dying day?
Am I to yield you to a rival's arms
And not console myself with other charms?
MARIANE.
Go then: console yourself; don't hesitate.
I wish you to; indeed, I cannot wait.
VALÈRE.
You wish me to?
MARIANE.

        Yes.
VALÈRE.

           That's the final straw.
Madam, farewell. Your wish shall be my law.
(He starts to leave, and then returns: this repeatedly:)
MARIANE.
Splendid.
VALÈRE. *(Coming back again.)*

       This breach, remember, is of your making;
It's you who've driven me to the step I'm taking.
MARIANE.
Of course.
VALÈRE. *(Coming back again.)*

       Remember, too, that I am merely
Following your example.
MARIANE.

        I see that clearly.

VALÈRE.
Enough. I'll go and do your bidding, then.

MARIANE.
Good.

VALÈRE. *(Coming back again.)*
        You shall never see my face again.

MARIANE.
Excellent.

VALÈRE. *(Walking to the door, then turning about.)*
                Yes?

MARIANE.
                        What?

VALÈRE.
                                What's that? What did you say?

MARIANE.
Nothing. You're dreaming.

VALÈRE.
                                Ah. Well, I'm on my way.

Farewell, *Madame.*
(He moves slowly away.)

MARIANE.
                        Farewell.

DORINE. *(To Mariane.)*
                                If you ask me,
Both of you are as mad as mad can be.
Do stop this nonsense, now. I've only let you
Squabble so long to see where it would get you.
Whoa there, Monsieur Valère!
(She goes and seizes Valère by the arm; he makes a great show of resistance.)

VALÈRE.
                        What's this, Dorine?

DORINE.
Come here.

VALÈRE.
                No, no, my heart's too full of spleen.
Don't hold me back; her wish must be obeyed.

DORINE.
Stop!
VALÈRE.
      It's too late now; my decision's made.
DORINE.
Oh, pooh!
MARIANE. *(Aside.)*
      He hates the sight of me, that's plain.
I'll go, and so deliver him from pain.
DORINE. *(Leaving Valère, running after Mariane.)*
And now *you* run away! Come back.
MARIANE.
                      No, no.
Nothing you say will keep me here. Let go!
VALÈRE. *(Aside.)*
She cannot bear my presence, I perceive.
To spare her further torment, I shall leave.
DORINE. *(Leaving Mariane, running after Valère.)*
Again! You'll not escape, Sir; don't you try it.
Come here, you two. Stop fussing, and be quiet.
(She takes Valère by the hand, then Mariane, and draws them together.)
VALÈRE. *(To Dorine.)*
What do you want of me?
MARIANE. *(To Dorine.)*
              What is the point of this?
DORINE.
We're going to have a little armistice.
(To Valère.)
Now, weren't you silly to get so overheated?
VALÈRE.
Didn't you see how badly I was treated?
DORINE. *(To Mariane.)*
Aren't you a simpleton, to have lost your head?
MARIANE.
Didn't you hear the hateful things he said?

47

DORINE. *(To Valère.)*
You're both great fools. Her sole desire, Valère,
Is to be yours in marriage. To that I'll swear.
(To Mariane.)
He loves you only, and he wants no wife
But you, Mariane. On that I'll stake my life.
MARIANE. *(To Valère.)*
Then why you advised me so, I cannot see.
VALÈRE. *(To Mariane.)*
On such a question, why ask advice of *me?*
DORINE. Oh, you're impossible. Give me your hands, you
two.
(To Valère.)
Yours first.
VALÈRE. *(Giving Dorine his hand.)*
        But why?
DORINE. *(To Mariane.)*
               And now a hand from you.
MARIANE. *(Also giving Dorine her hand.)*
What are you doing?
DORINE.
           There: a perfect fit.
You suit each other better than you'll admit.
*(Valère and Mariane hold hands for some time without looking at
each other.)*
VALÈRE. *(Turning toward Mariane.)*
Ah, come, don't be so haughty. Give a man
A look of kindness, won't you, Mariane?
(Mariane turns toward Valère and smiles.)
DORINE.
I tell you, lovers are completely mad!
VALÈRE. *(To Mariane.)*
Now come, confess that you were very bad
To hurt my feelings as you did just now.
I have a just complaint, you must allow.

MARIANE.
You must allow that you were most unpleasant...
DORINE.
Let's table that discussion for the present;
Your father has a plan which must be stopped.
MARIANE.
Advise us, then; what means must we adopt?
DORINE.
We'll use all manner of means, and all at once.
(To Mariane.)
Your father's addled; he's acting like a dunce.
Therefore you'd better humor the old fossil.
Pretend to yield to him, be sweet and docile,
And then postpone, as often as necessary,
The day on which you have agreed to marry.
You'll thus gain time, and time will turn the trick.
Sometimes, for instance, you'll be taken sick,
And that will seem good reason for delay;
Or some bad omen will make you change the day—
You'll dream of muddy water, or you'll pass
A dead man's hearse, or break a looking-glass.
If all else fails, no man can marry you
Unless you take his ring and say "I do."
But now, let's separate. If they should find
Us talking here, our plot might be divined.
(To Valère.)
Go to your friends, and tell them what's occurred,
And have them urge her father to keep his word.
Meanwhile, we'll stir her brother into action,
And get Elmire, as well, to join our faction.
Good-bye.
VALÈRE. *(To Mariane.)*
                Though each of us will do his best,
It's your true heart on which my hopes shall rest.
MARIANE. *(To Valère.)*
Regardless of what Father may decide,
None but Valère shall claim me as his bride.

VALÈRE.
Oh, how those words content me! Come what will...
DORINE. Oh, lovers, lovers! Their tongues are never still.
Be off, now.
VALÈRE.   *(Turning to go, then turning back.)*
                    One last word...
DORINE.
                              No time to chat:
You leave by this door; and *you* leave by that.
(Dorine pushes them, by the shoulders, toward opposing doors.)

ACT III
SCENE ONE

DAMIS, DORINE

DAMIS.
May lightning strike me even as I speak,
May all men call me cowardly and weak,
If any fear or scruple holds me back
From settling things, at once, with that great quack!
DORINE.
Now, don't give way to violent emotion.
Your father's merely talked about this notion,
And words and deeds are far from being one.
Much that is talked about is left undone.
DAMIS.
No, I must stop that scoundrel's machinations;
I'll go and tell him off; I'm out of patience.
DORINE.
Do calm down and be practical. I had rather
My mistress dealt with him—and with your father.
She has some influence with Tartuffe, I've noted.
He hangs upon her words, seems most devoted,
And may, indeed, be smitten by her charm.
Pray Heaven it's true! 'Twould do our cause no harm.
She sent for him, just now, to sound him out
On this affair you're so incensed about;
She'll find out where he stands, and tell him, too,
What dreadful strife and trouble will ensue
If he lends countenance to your father's plan.

51

I couldn't get in to see him, but his man
Says that he's almost finished with his prayers.
Go, now. I'll catch him when he comes downstairs.
DAMIS.
I want to hear this conference, and I will.
DORINE.
No, they must be alone.
DAMIS.

                    Oh, I'll keep still.

DORINE.
Not you. I know your temper. You'd start a brawl,
And shout and stamp your foot and spoil it all.
Go on.
DAMIS.

      I won't; I have a perfect right...

DORINE.
Lord, you're a nuisance! He's coming; get out of sight.
(Damis conceals himself in a closet at the rear of the stage.)

SCENE TWO

TARTUFFE, DORINE

TARTUFFE. *(Observing Dorine, and calling to his manservant offstage.)*
Hang up my hair-shirt, put my scourge in place,
And pray, Laurent, for Heaven's perpetual grace.
I'm going to the prison now, to share
My last few coins with the poor wretches there.
DORINE. *(Aside.)*
Dear God, what affectation! What a fake!
TARTUFFE.
You wished to see me?

DORINE.

Yes...

TARTUFFE. *(Taking a handkerchief from his pocket.)*

For mercy's sake,
Please take this handkerchief, before you speak.

DORINE.

What?

TARTUFFE.

Cover that bosom, girl. The flesh is weak,
And unclean thoughts are difficult to control.
Such sights as that can undermine the soul.

DORINE.

Your soul, it seems, has very poor defenses,
And flesh makes quite an impact on your senses.
It's strange that you're so easily excited;
My own desires are not so soon ignited,
And if I saw you naked as a beast,
Not all your hide would tempt me in the least.

TARTUFFE.

Girl, speak more modestly; unless you do,
I shall be forced to take my leave of you.

DORINE.

Oh, no, it's I who must be on my way;
I've just one little message to convey.
Madame is coming down, and begs you, Sir,
To wait and have a word or two with her.

TARTUFFE.

Gladly.

DORINE. *(Aside.)*

That had a softening effect!
I think my guess about him was correct.

TARTUFFE.

Will she be long?

DORINE.

No: that's her step I hear.
Ah, here she is, and I shall disappear.

SCENE THREE

TARTUFFE.
May Heaven, whose infinite goodness we adore,
Preserve your body and soul forevermore,
And bless your days, and answer thus the plea
Of one who is its humblest votary.
ELMIRE.
I thank you for that pious wish. But please,
Do take a chair and let's be more at ease.
(They sit down.)
TARTUFFE.
I trust that you are once more well and strong?
ELMIRE.
Oh, yes: the fever didn't last for long.
TARTUFFE.
My prayers are too unworthy, I am sure,
To have gained from Heaven this most gracious cure;
But lately, Madam, my every supplication
Has had for object your recuperation.
ELMIRE.
You shouldn't have troubled so. I don't deserve it.
TARTUFFE.
Your health is priceless, Madam, and to preserve it
I'd gladly give my own, in all sincerity.
ELMIRE.
Sir, you outdo us all in Christian charity.
You've been most kind. I count myself your debtor.

TARTUFFE.
'Twas nothing, Madam. I long to serve you better.
ELMIRE.
There's a private matter I'm anxious to discuss.
I'm glad there's no one here to hinder us.
TARTUFFE.
I too am glad; it floods my heart with bliss
To find myself alone with you like this.
For just this chance I've prayed with all my power—
But prayed in vain, until this happy hour.
ELMIRE.
This won't take long, Sir, and I hope you'll be
Entirely frank and unconstrained with me.
TARTUFFE.
Indeed, there's nothing I had rather do
Than bare my inmost heart and soul to you.
First, let me say that what remarks I've made
About the constant visits you are paid
Were prompted not by any mean emotion,
But rather by a pure and deep devotion,
A fervent zeal...
ELMIRE.

        No need for explanation.
Your sole concern, I'm sure, was my salvation.
TARTUFFE. *(Taking Elmire's hand and pressing her fingertips.)*
Quite so; and such great fervor do I feel...
ELMIRE.
Ooh! Please! You're pinching!
TARTUFFE.

               'Twas from excess of zeal.
I never meant to cause you pain, I swear.
I'd rather...
(He places his hand on Elmire's knee.)
ELMIRE.

        What can your hand be doing there?
TARTUFFE. Feeling your gown; what soft, fine-woven stuff!

ELMIRE.

Please, I'm extremely ticklish. That's enough.

(She draws her chair away; Tartuffe pulls his after her.)

TARTUFFE. *(Fondling the lace collar of her gown.)*

My, my, what lovely lacework on your dress!

The workmanship's miraculous, no less.

I've not seen anything to equal it.

ELMIRE.

Yes, quite. But let's talk business for a bit.

They say my husband means to break his word

And give his daughter to you, Sir. Had you heard?

TARTUFFE.

He did once mention it. But I confess

I dream of quite a different happiness.

It's elsewhere, Madam, that my eyes discern

The promise of that bliss for which I yearn.

ELMIRE.

I see: you care for nothing here below.

TARTUFFE.

Ah, well—my heart's not made of stone, you know.

ELMIRE.

All your desires mount heavenward, I'm sure,

In scorn of all that's earthly and impure.

TARTUFFE.

A love of heavenly beauty does not preclude

A proper love for earthly pulchritude;

Our senses are quite rightly captivated

By perfect works our Maker has created.

Some glory clings to all that Heaven has made;

In you, all Heaven's marvels are displayed.

On that fair face, such beauties have been lavished,

The eyes are dazzled and the heart is ravished;

How could I look on you, O flawless creature,

And not adore the Author of all Nature,

Feeling a love both passionate and pure

For you, his triumph of self-portaiture?

At first, I trembled lest that love should be
A subtle snare that Hell had laid for me;
I vowed to flee the sight of you, eschewing
A rapture that might prove my soul's undoing;
But soon, fair being, I became aware
That my deep passion could be made to square
With rectitude, and with my bounden duty.
I thereupon surrendered to your beauty.
It is, I know, presumptuous on my part
To bring you this poor offering of my heart,
And it is not my merit, Heaven knows,
But your compassion on which my hopes repose.
You are my peace, my solace, my salvation;
On you depends my bliss—or desolation;
I bide your judgement and, as you think best,
I shall be either miserable or blest.

ELMIRE.

Your declaration is most gallant, Sir,
But don't you think it's out of character?
You'd have done better to restrain your passion
And think before you spoke in such a fashion.
It ill becomes a pious man like you...

TARTUFFE.

I may be pious, but I'm human too:
With your celestial charms before his eyes,
A man has not the power to be wise.
I know such words sound strangely, coming from me,
But I'm no angel, nor was meant to be,
And if you blame my passion, you must needs
Reproach as well the charms on which it feeds.
Your loveliness I had no sooner seen
Than you became my soul's unrivalled queen;
Before your seraph glance, divinely sweet,
My heart's defenses crumbled in defeat,
And nothing fasting, prayer, or tears might do
Could stay my spirit from adoring you.

My eyes, my sighs have told you in the past
What now my lips make bold to say at last,
And if, in your great goodness, you will deign
To look upon your slave, and ease his pain,—
If, in compassion for my soul's distress,
You'll stoop to comfort my unworthiness,
I'll raise to you, in thanks for that sweet manna,
And endless hymn, an infinite hosanna.
With me, of course, there need be no anxiety,
No fear of scandal or of notoriety.
These young court gallants, whom all the ladies fancy,
Are vain in speech, in action rash and chancy;
When they succeed in love, the world soon knows it;
No favor's granted them but they disclose it
And by the looseness of their tongues profane
The very altar where their hearts have lain.
Men of my sort, however, love discreetly,
And one may trust our reticence completely.
My keen concern for my good name insures
The absolute security of yours;
In short, I offer you, my dear Elmire,
Love without scandal, pleasure without fear.
ELMIRE.
I've heard your well-turned speeches to the end,
And what you urge I clearly apprehend.
Aren't you afraid that I may take a notion
To tell my husband of your warm devotion,
And that, supposing he were duly told,
His feeling toward you might grow rather cold?
TARTUFFE.
I know, dear lady, that your exceeding charity
Will lead your heart to pardon my temerity;
That you'll excuse my violent affection
As human weakness, human imperfection;
And that—O fairest!—you will bear in mind
That I'm but flesh and blood, and am not blind.

ELMIRE.

Some women might do otherwise, perhaps,
But I shall be discreet about your lapse;
I'll tell my husband nothing of what's occurred
If, in return, you'll give your solemn word
To advocate as forcefully as you can
The marriage of Valère and Mariane,
Renouncing all desire to dispossess
Another of his rightful happiness,
And...

SCENE FOUR

DAMIS, ELMIRE, TARTUFFE

DAMIS. *(Emerging from the closet where he has been hiding.)*
       No! We'll not hush up this vile affair;
I heard it all inside that closet there,
Where Heaven, in order to confound the pride
Of this great rascal, prompted me to hide.
Ah, now I have my long-awaited chance
To punish his deceit and arrogance,
And give my father clear and shocking proof
Of the black character of his dear Tartuffe.
ELMIRE.

Ah no, Damis; I'll be content if he
Will study to deserve my leniency.
I've promised silence—don't make me break my word;
To make a scandal would be too absurd.
Good wives laugh off such trifles, and forget them;
Why should they tell their husbands, and upset them?
DAMIS.

You have your reasons for taking such a course,

And I have reasons, too, of equal force.
To spare him now would be insanely wrong.
I've swallowed my just wrath for far too long
And watched this insolent bigot bringing strife
And bitterness into our family life.
Too long he's meddled in my father's affairs,
Thwarting my marriage-hopes, and poor Valère's.
It's high time that my father was undeceived,
And now I've proof that can't be disbelieved—
Proof that was furnished me by Heaven above.
It's too good not to take advantage of.
This is my chance, and I deserve to lose it
If, for one moment, I hesitate to use it.
ELMIRE.
Damis...
DAMIS.

        No, I must do what I think right.
Madam, my heart is bursting with delight,
And, say whatever you will, I'll not consent
To lose the sweet revenge on which I'm bent.
I'll settle matters without more ado;
And here, most opportunely, is my cue.

SCENE FIVE

ORGON, DAMIS, TARTUFFE, ELMIRE

DAMIS.
Father, I'm glad you've joined us. Let us advise you
Of some fresh news which doubtless will surprise you.
You've just now been repaid with interest
For all your loving-kindness to our guest.
He's proved his warm and grateful feelings toward you;

60

It's with a pair of horns he would reward you.
Yes, I surprised him with your wife, and heard
His whole adulterous offer, every word.
She, with her all too gentle disposition,
Would not have told you of his proposition;
But I shall not make terms with brazen lechery,
And feel that not to tell you would be treachery.
ELMIRE.
And I hold that one's husband's peace of mind
Should not be spoilt by tattle of this kind.
One's honor doesn't require it: to be proficent
In keeping men at bay is quite sufficient.
These are my sentiments, and I wish, Damis,
That you had heeded me and held your peace.

SCENE SIX

ORGON, DAMIS, TARTUFFE

ORGON.
Can it be true, this dreadful thing I hear?
TARTUFFE.
Yes, Brother, I'm a wicked man, I fear:
A wretched sinner, all depraved and twisted,
The greatest villain that has ever existed.
My life's one heap of crimes, which grows each minute;
There's naught but foulness and corruption in it;
And I perceive that Heaven, outraged by me,
Has chosen this occasion to mortify me.
Charge me with any deed you wish to name;
I'll not defend myself, but take the blame.
Believe what you are told, and drive Tartuffe
Like some base criminal from beneath your roof;

61

Yes, drive me hence, and with a parting curse:
I shan't protest, for I deserve far worse.
ORGON. *(To Damis.)*
Ah, you deceitful boy, how dare you try
To stain his purity with so foul a lie?
DAMIS.
What! Are you taken in by such a bluff?
Did you not hear...?
ORGON.

                              Enough, you rogue, enough!

TARTUFFE.
Ah, Brother, let him speak: you're being unjust.
Believe his story; the boy deserves your trust.
Why, after all, should you have faith in me?
How can you know what I might do, or be?
Is it on my good actions that you base
Your favor? Do you trust my pious face?
Ah, no, don't be deceived by hollow shows;
I'm far, alas, from being what men suppose;
Though the world takes me for a man of worth,
I'm truly the most worthless man on earth.
(To Damis.)
Yes, my dear son, speak out now: call me the chief
Of sinners, a wretch, a murderer, a thief;
Load me with all the names men most abhor;
I'll not complain; I've earned them all, and more;
I'll kneel here while you pour them on my head.
As a just punishment for the life I've led.
ORGON. *(To Tartuffe.)*
This is too much, dear Brother.
(To Damis.)

                              Have you no heart?

DAMIS.
Are you so hoodwinked by this rascal's art...?
ORGON.
Be still, you monster.

(To Tartuffe.)

                    Brother, I pray you, rise.

(To Damis.)
Villain!
DAMIS.

          But...
ORGON.

                Silence!

DAMIS.

                    Can't you realize...?

ORGON.

Just one word more, and I'll tear you limb from limb.
TARTUFFE.

In God's name, Brother, don't be harsh with him.
I'd rather far be tortured at the stake
Than see him bear one scratch for my poor sake.
ORGON. *(To Damis.)*

Ingrate!
TARTUFFE.

          If I must beg you, on bended knee,
To pardon him...
ORGON. *(Falling to his knees, addressing Tartuffe.)*

                    Such goodness cannot be!
(To Damis.)
Now, *there's* true charity!
DAMIS.

                    What, you...?

ORGON.

                              Villain, be still!
I know your motives; I know you wish him ill:
Yes, all of you—wife, children, servants, all—
Conspire against him and desire his fall,
Employing every shameful trick you can
To alienate me from this saintly man.
Ah, but the more you seek to drive him away,
The more I'll do to keep him. Without delay,

I'll spite this household and confound its pride
By giving him my daughter as his bride.
DAMIS.
You're going to force her to accept his hand?
ORGON.
Yes, and this very night, d'you understand?
I shall defy you all, and make it clear
That I'm the one who gives the orders here.
Come, wretch, kneel down and clasp his blessed feet,
And ask his pardon for your black deceit.
DAMIS.
I ask that swindler's pardon? Why, I'd rather...
ORGON.
So! You insult him, and defy your father!
A stick! A stick!
(To Tartuffe.)
                    No, no—release me, do.

(To Damis.)
Out of my house this minute! Be off with you,
And never dare set foot in it again.
DAMIS.
Well, I shall go, but...
ORGON.
                  Well, go quickly, then.

I disinherit you; an empty purse
Is all you'll get from me—except my curse!

SCENE SEVEN

ORGON, TARTUFFE

ORGON.
How he blasphemed your goodness! What a son!

TARTUFFE.

Forgive him, Lord, as I've already done.
(To Orgon.)
You can't know how it hurts when someone tries
To blacken me in my dear Brother's eyes.
ORGON.

Ahh!
TARTUFFE.

      The mere thought of such ingratitude
Plunges my soul into so dark a mood...
Such horror grips my heart...I gasp for breath,
And cannot speak, and feel myself near death.
ORGON. *(He runs, in tears, to the door through which he has just driven his son.)*
You blackguard! Why did I spare you? Why did I not
Break you in little pieces on the spot?
Compose yourself, and don't be hurt, dear friend.
TARTUFFE.

These scenes, these dreadful quarrels, have got to end.
I've much upset your household, and I perceive
That the best thing will be for me to leave.
ORGON.

What are you saying!
TARTUFFE.

               They're all against me here:
They'd have you think me false and insincere.
ORGON.

Ah, what of that? Have I ceased believing in you?
TARTUFFE.

Their adverse talk will certainly continue,
And charges which you now repudiate
You may find credible at a later date.
ORGON.

No, Brother, never.
TARTUFFE.

           Brother, a wife can sway
Her husband's mind in many a subtle way.

ORGON.
No, no.
TARTUFFE.

      To leave at once is the solution;
Thus only can I end their persecution.
ORGON.
No, no, I'll not allow it; you shall remain.
TARTUFFE.
Ah, well; 'twill mean much martyrdom and pain,
But if you wish it...
ORGON.

          Ah!

TARTUFFE.

          Enough; so be it.
But one thing must be settled, as I see it.
For your dear honor, and for our friendship's sake,
There's one precaution I feel bound to take.
I shall avoid your wife, and keep away...
ORGON.
No, you shall not, whatever they may say.
It pleases me to vex them, and for spite
I'd have them see you with her day and night.
What's more, I'm going to drive them to despair
By making you my only son and heir;
This very day, I'll give to you alone
Clear deed and title to everything I own.
A dear, good friend and son-in-law-to-be
Is more than wife, or child, or kin to me.
Will you accept my offer, dearest son?
TARTUFFE.
In all things, let the will of Heaven be done.
ORGON.
Poor fellow! Come, we'll go draw up the deed.
Then let them burst with disappointed greed!

ACT IV
SCENE ONE

CLÉANTE, TARTUFFE

CLÉANTE.
Yes, all the town's discussing it, and truly,
Their comments do not flatter you unduly.
I'm glad we've met, Sir, and I'll give my view
Of this sad matter in a word or two.
As for who's guilty, that I shan't discuss;
Let's say it was Damis who caused the fuss;
Assuming, then, that you have been ill-used
By young Damis, and groundlessly accused,
Ought not a Christian to forgive, and ought
He not to stifle every vengeful thought?
Should you stand by and watch a father make
His only son an exile for your sake?
Again I tell you frankly, be advised:
The whole town, high and low, is scandalized;
This quarrel must be mended, and my advice is
Not to push matters to a further crisis.
No, sacrifice your wrath to God above,
And help Damis regain his father's love.
TARTUFFE.
Alas, for my part I should take great joy
In doing so. I've nothing against the boy.
I pardon all, I harbor no resentment;
To serve him would afford me much contentment.
But Heaven's interest will not have it so:

If he comes back, then I shall have to go.
After his conduct—so extreme, so vicious—
Our further intercourse would look suspicious.
God knows what people would think! Why, they'd describe
My goodness to him as a sort of bribe;
They'd say that out of guilt I made pretense
Of loving-kindness and benevolence—
That, fearing my accuser's tongue, I strove
To buy his silence with a show of love.

CLÉANTE.
Your reasoning is badly warped and stretched,
And these excuses, Sir, are most far-fetched.
Why put yourself in charge of Heaven's cause?
Does Heaven need our help to enforce its laws?
Leave vengeance to the Lord, Sir; while we live,
Our duty's not to punish, but forgive;
And what the Lord commands, we should obey
Without regard to what the world may say.
What! Shall the fear of being misunderstood
Prevent our doing what is right and good?
No, no, let's simply do what Heaven ordains,
And let no other thoughts perplex our brains.

TARTUFFE.
Again, Sir, let me say that I've forgiven
Damis, and thus obeyed the laws of Heaven;
But I am not commanded by the Bible
To live with one who smears my name with libel.

CLEANTE.
Were you commanded, Sir, to indulge the whim
Of poor Orgon, and to encourage him
In suddenly transferring to your name
A large estate to which you have no claim?

TARTUFFE.
'Twould never occur to those who know me best
To think I acted from self-interest.
The treasures of this world I quite despise;
Their specious glitter does not charm my eyes;

And if I have resigned myself to taking
The gift which my dear Brother insists on making,
I do so only, as he well understands,
Lest so much wealth fall into wicked hands,
Lest those to whom it might descend in time
Turn it to purposes of sin and crime,
And not, as I shall do, make use of it
For Heaven's glory and mankind's benefit.
CLÉANTE.

Forget these trumped-up fears. Your argument
Is one the rightful heir might well resent;
It *is* a moral burden to inherit
Such wealth, but give Damis a chance to bear it.
And would it not be worse to be accused
Of swindling, than to see that wealth misused?
I'm shocked that you allowed Orgon to broach
This matter, and that you feel no self-reproach;
Does true religion teach that lawful heirs
May freely be deprived of what is theirs?
And if the Lord has told you in your heart
That you and young Damis must dwell apart,
Would it not be the decent thing to beat
A generous and honorable retreat,
Rather than let the son of the house be sent,
For your convenience, into banishment?
Sir, if you wish to prove the honesty
Of your intentions...
TARTUFFE.

                              Sir, it is half-past three.
I've certain pious duties to attend to,
And hope my prompt departure won't offend you.
CLÉANTE. *(Alone.)*
Damn.

69

SCENE TWO

ELMIRE, MARIANE, CLÉANTE, DORINE

DORINE.
    Stay, Sir, and help Mariane, for Heaven's sake!
She's suffering so, I fear her heart will break.
Her father's plan to marry her off tonight
Has put the poor child in a desperate plight.
I hear him coming. Let's stand together, now,
And see if we can't change his mind, somehow,
About this match we all deplore and fear.

SCENE THREE

ORGON, ELMIRE, MARIANE, CLÉANTE, DORINE

ORGON.
Hah! Glad to find you all assembled here.
(To Mariane.)
This contract, child, contains your happiness,
And what it says I think your heart can guess.
MARIANE. *(Falling to her knees.)*
Sir, by that Heaven which sees me here distressed,
And by whatever else can move your breast,
Do not employ a father's power, I pray you,
To crush my heart and force it to obey you,

70

Nor by your harsh commands oppress me so
That I'll begrudge the duty which I owe—
And do not so embitter and enslave me
That I shall hate the very life you gave me.
If my sweet hopes must perish, if you refuse
To give me to the one I've dared to choose,
Spare me at least — I beg you, I implore—
The pain of wedding one whom I abhor;
And do not, by a heartless use of force,
Drive me to contemplate some desperate course.
ORGON. *(Feeling himself touched by her.)*
Be firm, my soul. No human weakness, now.
MARIANE.
I don't resent your love for him. Allow
Your heart free rein, Sir; give him your property,
And if that's not enough, take mine from me;
He's welcome to my money; take it, do,
But don't, I pray, include my person too.
Spare me, I beg you; and let me end the tale
Of my sad days behind a convent veil.
ORGON.
A convent! Hah! When crossed in their amours,
All lovesick girls have the same thought as yours.
Get up! The more you loathe the man, and dread him,
The more ennobling it will be to wed him.
Marry Tartuffe, and mortify your flesh!
Enough; don't start that whimpering afresh.
DORINE.
But why...?
ORGON.

       Be still, there. Speak when you're spoken to.
Not one more bit of impudence out of you.
CLEANTE.
If I may offer a word of counsel here...
ORGON.
Brother, in counseling you have no peer;

All your advice is forceful, sound, and clever;
I don't propose to follow it, however.
ELMIRE. *(To Orgon.)*
I am amazed, and don't know what to say;
Your blindness simply takes my breath away.
You are indeed bewitched, to take no warning
From our account of what occurred this morning.
ORGON.
Madam, I know a few plain facts, and one
Is that you're partial to my rascal son;
Hence, when he sought to make Tartuffe the victim
Of a base lie, you dared not contradict him.
Ah, but you underplayed your part, my pet;
You should have looked more angry, more upset.
ELMIRE.
When men make overtures, must we reply
With righteous anger and a battle-cry?
Must we turn back their amorous advances
With sharp reproaches and with fiery glances?
Myself, I find such offers merely amusing,
And make no scenes and fusses in refusing;
My taste is for good-natured rectitude,
And I dislike the savage sort of prude
Who guards her virtue with her teeth and claws,
And tears men's eyes out for the slightest cause:
The Lord preserve me from such honor as that,
Which bites and scratches like an alley-cat!
I've found that a polite and cool rebuff
Discourages a lover quite enough.
ORGON.
I know the facts, and I shall not be shaken.
ELMIRE.
I marvel at your power to be mistaken.
Would it, I wonder, carry weight with you
If I could *show* you that our tale was true?

ORGON.
Show me?
ELMIRE.
    Yes.
ORGON.
      Rot.
ELMIRE.
         Come, what if I found a way
To make you see the facts as plain as day?
ORGON.
Nonsense.
ELMIRE.
      Do answer me; don't be absurd.
I'm not now asking you to trust our word.
Suppose that from some hiding-place in here
You learned the whole sad truth by eye and ear—
What would you say of your good friend, after that?
ORGON.
Why, I'd say...nothing, by Jehoshaphat!
It can't be true.
ELMIRE.
        You've been too long deceived,
And I'm quite tired of being disbelieved.
Come now: let's put my statements to the test,
And you shall see the truth made manifest.
ORGON.
I'll take that challenge. Now do your uttermost.
We'll see how you make good your empty boast.
ELMIRE. *(To Dorine.)*
Send him to me.
DORINE.
      He's crafty; it may be hard
To catch the cunning scoundrel off his guard.
ELMIRE.
No, amorous men are gullible. Their conceit

So blinds them that they're never hard to cheat.
Have him come down.
(To Cléante and Mariane.)

Please leave us, for a bit.

SCENE FOUR

ELMIRE, ORGON

ELMIRE.
Pull up this table, and get under it.
ORGON.
What?
ELMIRE.
It's essential that you be well-hidden.
ORGON.
Why there?
ELMIRE.
Oh, Heavens! Just do as you are bidden.
I have my plans; we'll soon see how they fare.
Under the table, now; and once you're there,
Take care that you are neither seen nor heard.
ORGON.
Well, I'll indulge you, since I gave my word
To see you through this infantile charade.
ELMIRE.
Once it is over, you'll be glad we played.
(To her husband, who is now under the table.)
I'm going to act quite strangely, now, and you
Must not be shocked at anything I do.
Whatever I may say, you must excuse
As part of that deceit I'm forced to use.
I shall employ sweet speeches in the task
Of making that impostei drop his mask;

74

I'll give encouragement to his bold desires,
And furnish fuel to his amorous fires.
Since it's for your sake, and for his destruction,
That I shall seem to yield to his seduction,
I'll gladly stop whenever you decide
That all your doubts are fully satisfied.
I'll count on you, as soon as you have seen
What sort of man he is, to intervene,
And not expose me to his odious lust
One moment longer than you feel you must.
Remember: you're to save me from my plight
Whenever...He's coming! Hush! Keep out of sight!

SCENE FIVE

TARTUFFE, ELMIRE, ORGON

TARTUFFE.
You wish to have a word with me, I'm told.
ELMIRE.
Yes. I've a little secret to unfold.
Before I speak, however, it would be wise
To close that door, and look about for spies.
(Tartuffe goes to the door, closes it, and returns.)
The very last thing that must happen now
Is a repetition of this morning's row.
I've never been so badly caught off guard.
Oh, how I feared for you! You saw how hard
I tried to make that troublesome Damis
Control his dreadful temper, and hold his peace.
In my confusion, I didn't have the sense
Simply to contradict his evidence;
But as it happened, that was for the best,

And all has worked out in our interest.
This storm has only bettered your position;
My husband doesn't have the least suspicion,
And now, in mockery of those who do,
He bids me be continually with you.
And that is why, quite fearless of reproof,
I now can be alone with my Tartuffe,
And why my heart—perhaps too quick to yield—
Feels free to let its passion be revealed.
TARTUFFE.
Madam, your words confuse me. Not long ago,
You spoke in quite a different style, you know.
ELMIRE.
Ah, Sir, if that refusal made you smart,
It's little that you know of woman's heart,
Or what that heart is trying to convey
When it resists in such a feeble way!
Always, at first, our modesty prevents
The frank avowal of tender sentiments;
However high the passion which inflames us,
Still, to confess its power somehow shames us.
Thus we reluct, at first, yet in a tone
Which tells you that our heart is overthrown,
That what our lips deny, our pulse confesses,
And that, in time, all noes will turn to yesses.
I fear my words are all too frank and free,
And a poor proof of woman's modesty;
But since I'm started, tell me, if you will—
Would I have tried to make Damis be still,
Would I have listened, calm and unoffended,
Until your lengthy offer of love was ended,
And been so very mild in my reaction,
Had your sweet words not given me satisfaction?
And when I tried to force you to undo
The marriage-plans my husband has in view,
What did my urgent pleading signify

76

If not that I admired you, and that I
Deplored the thought that someone else might own
Part of a heart I wished for mine alone?
TARTUFFE.
Madam, no happiness is so complete
As when, from lips we love, come words so sweet;
Their nectar floods my every sense, and drains
In honeyed rivulets through all my veins.
To please you is my joy, my only goal;
Your love is the restorer of my soul;
And yet I must beg leave, now, to confess
Some lingering doubts as to my happiness.
Might this not be a trick? Might not the catch
Be that you wish me to break off the match
With Mariane, and so have feigned to love me?
I shan't quite trust your fond opinion of me
Until the feelings you've expressed so sweetly
Are demonstrated somewhat more concretely,
And you have shown, by certain kind concessions,
That I may put my faith in your professions.
ELMIRE. *(She coughs, to warn her husband.)*
Why be in such a hurry? Must my heart
Exhaust its bounty at the very start?
To make that sweet admission cost me dear,
But you'll not be content, it would appear,
Unless my store of favors is disbursed
To the last farthing, and at the very first.
TARTUFFE.
The less we merit, the less we dare to hope,
And with our doubts, mere words can never cope.
We trust no promised bliss till we receive it;
Not till a joy is ours can we believe it.
I, who so little merit your esteem,
Can't credit this fulfillment of my dream,
And shan't believe it, Madam, until I savor
Some palpable assurance of your favor.

77

ELMIRE.

My, how tyrannical your love can be,
And how it flusters and perplexes me!
How furiously you take one's heart in hand,
And make your every wish a fierce command!
Come, must you hound and harry me to death?
Will you not give me time to catch my breath?
Can it be right to press me with such force,
Give me no quarter, show me no remorse,
And take advantage, by your stern insistence,
Of the fond feelings which weaken my resistance?

TARTUFFE.

Well, if you look with favor upon my love,
Why, then, begrudge me some clear proof thereof?

ELMIRE.

But how can I consent without offense
To Heaven, toward which you feel such reverence?

TARTUFFE.

If Heaven is all that holds you back, don't worry.
I can remove that hindrance in a hurry.
Nothing of that sort need obstruct our path.

ELMIRE.

Must one not be afraid of Heaven's wrath?

TARTUFFE.

Madam, forget such fears, and be my pupil,
And I shall teach you how to conquer scruple.
Some joys, it's true, are wrong in Heaven's eyes;
Yet Heaven is not averse to compromise;
There is a science, lately formulated,
Whereby one's conscience may be liberated,
And any wrongful act you care to mention
May be redeemed by purity of intention.
I'll teach you, Madam, the secrets of that science;
Meanwhile, just place on me your full reliance.
Assuage my keen desires, and feel no dread:
The sin, if any, shall be on my head.

(Elmire coughs, this time more loudly.)
You've a bad cough.
ELMIRE.

Yes, yes. It's bad indeed.
TARTUFFE. *(Producing a little paper bag.)*
A bit of licorice may be what you need.
ELMIRE.
No, I've a stubborn cold, it seems. I'm sure it
Will take much more than licorice to cure it.
TARTUFFE.
How aggravating.
ELMIRE.

Oh, more than I can say.
TARTUFFE.
If you're still troubled, think of things this way:
No one shall know our joys, save us alone,
And there's no evil till the act is known;
It's scandal, Madam, which makes it an offense,
And it's no sin to sin in confidence.
ELMIRE. *(Having coughed once more.)*
Well, clearly I must do as you require,
And yield to your importunate desire.
It is apparent, now, that nothing less
Will satisfy you, and so I acquiesce.
To go so far is much against my will;
I'm vexed that it should come to this; but still,
Since you are so determined on it, since you
Will not allow mere language to convince you,
And since you ask for concrete evidence, I
See nothing for it, now, but to comply.
If this is sinful, if I'm wrong to do it,
So much the worse for him who drove me to it.
The fault can surely not be charged to me.
TARTUFFE.
Madam, the fault is mine, if fault there be,
And...

ELMIRE.

Open the door a little, and peek out;
I wouldn't want my husband poking about.

TARTUFFE.

Why worry about the man? Each day he grows
More gullible; one can lead him by the nose.
To find us here would fill him with delight,
And if he saw the worst, he'd doubt his sight.

ELMIRE.

Nevertheless, do step out for a minute
Into the hall, and see that no one's in it.

SCENE SIX

ORGON, ELMIRE

ORGON. *(Coming out from under the table.)*
That man's a perfect monster, I must admit!
I'm simply stunned. I can't get over it.

ELMIRE.

What, coming out so soon? How premature!
Get back in hiding, and wait until you're sure.
Stay till the end, and be convinced completely;
We mustn't stop till things are proved concretely.

ORGON.

Hell never harbored anything so vicious!

ELMIRE.

Tut, don't be hasty. Try to be judicious.
Wait, and be certain that there's no mistake.
No jumping to conclusions, for Heaven's sake!
(She places Orgon behind her, as Tartuffe re-enters.)

SCENE SEVEN

TARTUFFE, ELMIRE, ORGON

TARTUFFE. *(Not seeing Orgon.)*
Madam, all things have worked out to perfection;
I've given the neighboring rooms a full inspection;
No one's about; and now I may at last...
ORGON. *(Intercepting him.)*
Hold on, my passionate fellow, not so fast!
I should advise a little more restraint.
Well, so you thought you'd fool me, my dear saint!
How soon you wearied of the saintly life—
Wedding my daughter, and coveting my wife!
I've long suspected you, and had a feeling
That soon I'd catch you at your double-dealing.
Just now, you've given me evidence galore;
It's quite enough; I have no wish for more.
ELMIRE. *(To Tartuffe.)*
I'm sorry to have treated you so slyly,
But circumstances forced me to be wily.
TARTUFFE.
Brother, you can't think...
ORGON.

                                        No more talk from you;
Just leave this household, without more ado.

TARTUFFE.
What I intended...
ORGON.

              That seems fairly clear.
Spare me your falsehoods and get out of here.
TARTUFFE.
No, I'm the master, and you're the one to go!
This house belongs to me, I'll have you know,
And I shall show you that you can't hurt *me*
By this contemptible conspiracy,
That those who cross me know not what they do,
And that I've means to expose and punish you,
Avenge offended Heaven, and make you grieve
That ever you dared order me to leave.

SCENE EIGHT

ELMIRE, ORGON

ELMIRE.
What was the point of all that angry chatter?
ORGON.
Dear God, I'm worried. This is no laughing matter.
ELMIRE.
How so?
ORGON.

       I fear I understood his drift.
I'm much disturbed about that deed of gift.
ELMIRE.
You gave him...?
ORGON.

           Yes, it's all been drawn and signed.
But one thing more is weighing on my mind.

ELMIRE.
What's that?
ORGON.

   I'll tell you; but first let's see if there's
A certain strong-box in his room upstairs.

ACT V
SCENE ONE

ORGON, CLÉANTE

CLÉANTE.
Where are you going so fast?
ORGON.

                              God knows!

CLÉANTE.

                              Then wait;
Let's have a conference, and deliberate
On how this situation's to be met.
ORGON.
That strong-box has me utterly upset;
This is the worst of many, many shocks.
CLÉANTE.
Is there some fearful mystery in that box?
ORGON.
My poor friend Argas brought that box to me
With his own hands, in utmost secrecy;
'Twas on the very morning of his flight.
It's full of papers which, if they came to light,
Would ruin him—or such is my impression.
CLÉANTE.
Then why did you let it out of your possession?
ORGON.
Those papers vexed my conscience, and it seemed best
To ask the counsel of my pious guest.
The cunning scoundrel got me to agree

To leave the strong-box in his custody,
So that, in case of an investigation,
I could employ a slight equivocation
And swear I didn't have it, and thereby,
At no expense to conscience, tell a lie.
CLÉANTE.
It looks to me as if you're out on a limb.
Trusting him with that box, and offering him
That deed of gift, were actions of a kind
Which scarcely indicate a prudent mind.
With two such weapons, he has the upper hand,
And since you're vulnerable, as matters stand,
You erred once more in bringing him to bay.
You should have acted in some subtler way.
ORGON.
Just think of it: behind that fervent face,
A heart so wicked, and a soul so base!
I took him in, a hungry beggar, and then...
Enough, by God! I'm through with pious men:
Henceforth I'll hate the whole false brotherhood,
And persecute them worse than Satan could.
CLÉANTE.
Ah, there you go—extravagant as ever!
Why can you not be rational? You never
Manage to take the middle course, it seems,
But jump, instead, between absurd extremes.
You've recognized your recent grave mistake
In falling victim to a pious fake;
Now, to correct that error, must you embrace
An even greater error in its place,
And judge our worthy neighbors as a whole
By what you've learned of one corrupted soul?
Come, just because one rascal made you swallow
A show of zeal which turned out to be hollow,
Shall you conclude that all men are deceivers,
And that, today, there are no true believers?

Let atheists make that foolish inference;
Learn to distinguish virtue from pretense,
Be cautious in bestowing admiration,
And cultivate a sober moderation.
Don't humor fraud, but also don't asperse
True piety; the latter fault is worse,
And it is best to err, if err one must,
As you have done, upon the side of trust.

SCENE TWO

DAMIS, ORGON, CLÉANTE

DAMIS.
Father, I hear that scoundrel's uttered threats
Against you; that he pridefully forgets
How, in his need, he was befriended by you,
And means to use your gifts to crucify you.
ORGON.
It's true, my boy. I'm too distressed for tears.
DAMIS.
Leave it to me, Sir; let me trim his ears.
Faced with such insolence, we must not waver.
I shall rejoice in doing you the favor
Of cutting short his life, and your distress.
CLÉANTE.
What a display of young hotheadedness!
Do learn to moderate your fits of rage.
In this just kingdom, this enlightened age,
One does not settle things by violence.

SCENE THREE

MADAME PERNELLE, MARIANE, ELMIRE,
DORINE, DAMIS, ORGON, CLÉANTE

MADAME PERNELLE.
I hear strange tales of very strange events.
ORGON.
Yes, strange events which these two eyes beheld.
The man's ingratitude is unparalleled.
I save a wretched pauper from starvation,
House him, and treat him like a blood relation,
Shower him every day with my largesse,
Give him my daughter, and all that I possess;
And meanwhile the unconscionable knave
Tries to induce my wife to misbehave;
And not content with such extreme rascality,
Now threatens me with my own liberality,
And aims, by taking base advantage of
The gifts I gave him out of Christian love,
To drive me from my house, a ruined man,
And make me end a pauper, as he began.
DORINE.
Poor fellow!
MADAME PERNELLE.
       No, my son, I'll never bring
Myself to think him guilty of such a thing.
ORGON.
How's that?
MADAME PERNELLE.
      The righteous always were maligned.

ORGON.

Speak clearly, Mother. Say what's on your mind.

MADAME PERNELLE.

I mean that I can smell a rat, my dear.
You know how everybody hates him, here.

ORGON.

That has no bearing on the case at all.

MADAME PERNELLE.

I told you a hundred times, when you were small,
That virtue in this world is hated ever;
Malicious men may die, but malice never.

ORGON.

No doubt that's true, but how does it apply?

MADAME PERNELLE.

They've turned you against him by a clever lie.

ORGON.

I've told you, I was there and saw it done.

MADAME PERNELLE.

Ah, slanderers will stop at nothing, Son.

ORGON.

Mother, I'll lose my temper...For the last time,
I tell you I was witness to the crime.

MADAME PERNELLE.

The tongues of spite are busy night and noon,
And to their venom no man is immune.

ORGON.

You're talking nonsense. Can't you realize
I saw it; saw it; saw it with my eyes?
Saw, do you understand me? Must I shout it
Into your ears before you'll cease to doubt it?

MADAME PERNELLE.

Appearances can deceive, my son. Dear me,
We cannot always judge by what we see.

ORGON.

Drat! Drat!

MADAME PERNELLE.

       One often interprets things awry;
Good can seem evil to a suspicious eye.

ORGON.

Was I to see his pawing at Elmire
As an act of charity?

MADAME PERNELLE.

             Till his guilt is clear,
A man deserves the benefit of the doubt.
You should have waited, to see how things turned out.

ORGON.

Great God in Heaven, what more proof did I need?
Was I to sit there, watching, until he'd...
You drive me to the brink of impropriety.

MADAME PERNELLE.

No, no, a man of such surpassing piety
Could not do such a thing. You cannot shake me.
I don't believe it, and you shall not make me.

ORGON.

You vex me so that, if you weren't my mother,
I'd say to you...some dreadful thing or other.

DORINE.

It's your turn now, Sir, not to be listened to;
You'd not trust us, and now she won't trust you.

CLÉANTE.

My friends, we're wasting time which should be spent
In facing up to our predicament.
I fear that scoundrel's threats weren't made in sport.

DAMIS.

Do you think he'd have the nerve to go to court?

ELMIRE.

I'm sure he won't: they'd find it all too crude
A case of swindling and ingratitude.

CLÉANTE.

Don't be too sure. He won't be at a loss
To give his claims a high and righteous gloss;

And clever rogues with far less valid cause
Have trapped their victims in a web of laws.
I say again that to antagonize
A man so strongly armed was most unwise.
ORGON.
I know it; but the man's appalling cheek
Outraged me so, I couldn't control my pique.
CLÉANTE.
I wish to Heaven that we could devise
Some truce between you, or some compromise.
ELMIRE.
If I had known what cards he held, I'd not
Have roused his anger by my little plot.
ORGON. *(To Dorine, as M. Loyal enters.)*
What is that fellow looking for? Who is he?
Go talk to him—and tell him that I'm busy.

SCENE FOUR

MONSIEUR LOYAL, MADAME PERNELLE, ORGON, DAMIS, MARIANE, DORINE, ELMIRE, CLÉANTE

MONSIEUR LOYAL.
Good day, dear sister. Kindly let me see
Your master.
DORINE.
              He's involved with company,
And cannot be disturbed just now, I fear.
MONSIEUR LOYAL.
I hate to intrude; but what has brought me here
Will not disturb your master, in any event.
Indeed, my news will make him most content.

DORINE.
Your name?
MONSIEUR LOYAL.

Just say that I bring greetings from
Monsieur Tartuffe, on whose behalf I've come.
DORINE. *(To Orgon.)*
Sir, he's a very gracious man, and bears
A message from Tartuffe, which, he declares,
Will make you most content.
CLÉANTE.

Upon my word,
I think this man had best be seen, and heard.
ORGON.
Perhaps he has some settlement to suggest.
How shall I treat him? What manner would be best?
CLÉANTE.
Control your anger, and if he should mention
Some fair adjustment, give him your full attention.
MONSIEUR LOYAL.
Good health to you, good Sir. May Heaven confound
Your enemies, and may your joys abound.
ORGON. *(Aside, to Cléante.)*
A gentle salutation: it confirms
My guess that he is here to offer terms.
MONSIEUR LOYAL.
I've always held your family most dear;
I served your father, Sir, for many a year.
ORGON.
Sir, I must ask your pardon; to my shame,
I cannot now recall your face or name.
MONSIEUR LOYAL.
Loyal's my name; I come from Normandy,
And I'm a bailiff, in all modesty.
For forty years, praise God, it's been my boast
To serve with honor in that vital post,
And I am here, Sir, if you will permit
The liberty, to serve you with this writ...

ORGON.
To—*what?*
MONSIEUR LOYAL.

     Now, please, Sir, let us have no friction:
It's nothing but an order of eviction.
You are to move your goods and family out
And make way for new occupants, without
Deferment or delay, and give the keys...
ORGON.
I? Leave this house?
MONSIEUR LOYAL.

          Why yes, Sir, if you please.
This house, Sir, from the cellar to the roof,
Belongs now to the good Monsieur Tartuffe,
And he is lord and master of your estate
By virtue of a deed of present date,
Drawn in due form, with clearest legal phrasing...
DAMIS.
Your insolence is utterly amazing!
MONSIEUR LOYAL.
Young man, my business here is not with you,
But with your wise and temperate father, who,
Like every worthy citizen, stands in awe
Of justice, and would never obstruct the law.
ORGON.
But...
MONSIEUR LOYAL.

    Not for a million, Sir, would you rebel
Against authority; I know that weil.
You'll not make trouble, Sir, or interfere
With the execution of my duties here.
DAMIS.
Someone may execute a smart tattoo
On that black jacket of yours, before you're through.
MONSIEUR LOYAL.
Sir, bid your son be silent. I'd much regret

Having to mention such a nasty threat
Of violence, in writing my report.
DORINE. *(Aside.)*
This man Loyal's a most disloyal sort!
MONSIEUR LOYAL.
I love all men of upright character,
And when I agreed to serve these papers, Sir,
It was your feelings that I had in mind.
I couldn't bear to see the case assigned
To someone else, who might esteem you less
And so subject you to unpleasantness.
ORGON.
What's more unpleasant than telling a man to leave
His house and home?
MONSIEUR LOYAL.
               You'd like a short reprieve?
If you desire it, Sir, I shall not press you,
But wait until tomorrow to dispossess you.
Splendid. I'll come and spend the night here, then,
Most quietly, with half a score of men.
For form's sake, you might bring me, just before
You go to bed, the keys to the front door.
My men, I promise, will be on their best
Behavior, and will not disturb your rest.
But bright and early, Sir, you must be quick
And move out all your furniture, every stick:
The men I've chosen are both young and strong,
And with their help it shouldn't take you long.
In short, I'll make things pleasant and convenient,
And since I'm being so extremely lenient,
Please show me, Sir, a like consideration,
And give me your entire cooperation.
ORGON. *(Aside.)*
I may be all but bankrupt, but I vow
I'd give a hundred louis, here and now,
Just for the pleasure of landing one good clout
Right on the end of that complacent snout.

CLÉANTE.
Careful; don't make things worse.
DAMIS.

My bootsole itches

To give that beggar a good kick in the breeches.
DORINE.
Monsieur Loyal, I'd love to hear the whack
Of a stout stick across your fine broad back.
MONSIEUR LOYAL.
Take care: a woman too may go to jail if
She uses threatening language to a bailiff.
CLÉANTE.
Enough, enough, Sir. This must not go on.
Give me that paper, please, and then begone.
MONSIEUR LOYAL.
Well, *au revoir*. God give you all good cheer!
ORGON.
May God confound you, and him who sent you here!

SCENE FIVE

ORGON, CLÉANTE, MARIANE, ELMIRE, MADAM.
PERNELLE, DORINE, DAMIS

ORGON.
Now, Mother, was I right or not? This writ
Should change your notion of Tartuffe a bit.
Do you perceive his villainy at last?
MADAME PERNELLE.
I'm thunderstruck. I'm utterly aghast.
DORINE.
Oh, come, be fair. You mustn't take offense
At this new proof of his benevolence.

He's acting out of selfless love, I know.
Material things enslave the soul, and so
He kindly has arranged your liberation
From all that might endanger your salvation.
ORGON.
Will you not ever hold your tongue, you dunce?
CLÉANTE.
Come, you must take some action, and at once.
ELMIRE.
Go tell the world of the low trick he's tried.
The deed of gift is surely nullified
By such behavior, and public rage will not
Permit the wretch to carry out his plot.

SCENE SIX

VALERE, ORGON, CLÉANTE, ELMIRE, MARIANE,
MADAME PERNELLE, DAMIS DORINE

VALÈRE.
Sir, though I hate to bring you more bad news,
Such is the danger that I cannot choose.
A friend who is extremely close to me
And knows my interest in your family
Has, for my sake, presumed to violate
The secrecy that's due to things of state,
And sends me word that you are in a plight
From which your one salvation lies in flight.
That scoundrel who's imposed upon you so
Denounced you to the King an hour ago
And, as supporting evidence, displayed
The strong-box of a certain renegade
Whose secret papers, so he testified,

95

You had disloyally agreed to hide.
I don't know just what charges may be pressed,
But there's a warrant out for your arrest;
Tartuffe has been instructed, furthermore,
To guide the arresting officer to your door.
CLÉANTE.
He's clearly done this to facilitate
His seizure of your house and your estate.
ORGON.
That man, I must say, is a vicious beast!
VALÈRE.
Quick, Sir; you mustn't tarry in the least.
My carriage is outside, to take you hence;
This thousand louis should cover all expense.
Let's lose no time, or you shall be undone;
The sole defense, in this case, is to run.
I shall go with you all the way, and place you
In a safe refuge to which they'll never trace you.
ORGON.
Alas, dear boy, I wish that I could show you
My gratitude for everything I owe you.
But now is not the time; I pray the Lord
That I may live to give you your reward.
Farewell, my dears; be careful...
CLÉANTE.

Brother, hurry.
We shall take care of things; you needn't worry.

SCENE SEVEN

*THE OFFICER, TARTUFFE, VALÈRE, ORGON,
ELMIRE, MARIANE, MADAME PERNELLE,
DORINE, CLÉANTE, DAMIS*

TARTUFFE.
Gently, Sir, gently; stay right where you are.
No need for haste; your lodging isn't far.
You're off to prison, by order of the Prince.
ORGON.
This is the crowning blow, you wretch; and since
It means my total ruin and defeat,
Your villainy is now at last complete.
TARTUFFE.
You needn't try to provoke me; it's no use.
Those who serve Heaven must expect abuse.
CLÉANTE.
You are indeed most patient, sweet, and blameless.
DAMIS.
How he exploits the name of Heaven! It's shameless.
TARTUFFE.
Your taunts and mockeries are all for naught;
To do my duty is my only thought.
MARIANE.
Your love of duty is most meritorious,
And what you've done is little short of glorious.
TARTUFFE.
All deeds are glorious, Madam, which obey
The sovereign prince who sent me here today.

ORGON.
I rescued you when you were destitute;
Have you forgotten that, you thankless brute?
TARTUFFE.
No, no, I well remember everything;
But my first duty is to serve my King.
That obligation is so paramount
That other claims, beside it, do not count;
And for it I would sacrifice my wife,
My family, my friend, or my own life.
ELMIRE.
Hypocrite!
DORINE.
   All that we most revere, he uses
To cloak his plots and camouflage his ruses.
CLÉANTE.
If it is true that you are animated
By pure and loyal zeal, as you have stated,
Why was this zeal not roused until you'd sought
To make Orgon a cuckold, and been caught?
Why weren't you moved to give your evidence
Until your outraged host had driven you hence?
I shan't say that the gift of all his treasure
Ought to have damped your zeal in any measure;
But if he is a traitor, as you declare,
How could you condescend to be his heir?
TARTUFFE. *(To the Officer.)*
Sir, spare me all this clamor; it's growing shrill.
Please carry out your orders, if you will.
OFFICER.
Yes, I've delayed too long, Sir. Thank you kindly.
You're just the proper person to remind me.
Come, you are off to join the other boarders
In the King's prison, according to his orders.
TARTUFFE.
Who? I, Sir?

OFFICER.
     Yes.
TARTUFFE.
          To prison? This can't be true!
OFFICER.
I owe an explanation, but not to you.
(To Orgon.)
Sir, all is well; rest easy, and be grateful.
We serve a Prince to whom all sham is hateful,
A Prince who sees into our inmost hearts,
And can't be fooled by any trickster's arts.
His royal soul, though generous and human,
Views all things with discernment and acumen;
His sovereign reason is not lightly swayed,
And all his judgments are discreetly weighed.
He honors righteous men of every kind,
And yet his zeal for virtue is not blind,
Nor does his love of piety numb his wits
And make him tolerant of hypocrites.
'Twas hardly likely that this man could cozen
A King who's foiled such liars by the dozen.
With one keen glance, the King perceived the whole
Perverseness and corruption of his soul,
And thus high Heaven's justice was displayed:
Betraying you, the rogue stood self-betrayed.
The King soon recognized Tartuffe as one
Notorious by another name, who'd done
So many vicious crimes that one could fill
Ten volumes with them, and be writing still.
But to be brief: our sovereign was appalled
By this man's treachery toward you, which he called
The last, worst villainy of a vile career,
And bade me follow the imposter here
To see how gross his impudence could be,
And force him to restore your property.
Your private papers, by the King's command,

I hereby seize and give into your hand.
The King, by royal order, invalidates
The deed which gave this rascal your estates,
And pardons, furthermore, your grave offense
In harboring an exile's documents.
By these decrees, our Prince rewards you for
Your loyal deeds in the late civil war,
And shows how heartfelt is his satisfaction
In recompensing any worthy action,
How much he prizes merit, and how he makes
More of men's virtues than of their mistakes.

DORINE.
Heaven be praised!

MADAME PERNELLE.

                        I breathe again, at last.

ELMIRE.
We're safe.

MARIANE.
        I can't believe the danger's past.

ORGON. *(To Tartuffe.)*
Well, traitor, now you see...

CLÉANTE.

                    Ah, Brother, please,
Let's not descend to such indignities.
Leave the poor wretch to his unhappy fate,
And don't say anything to aggravate
His present woes; but rather hope that he
Will soon embrace an honest piety,
And mend his ways, and by a true repentance
Move our just King to moderate his sentence.
Meanwhile, go kneel before your sovereign's throne
And thank him for the mercies he has shown.

ORGON.
Well said: let's go at once and, gladly kneeling,
Express the gratitude which all are feeling.
Then, when that first great duty has been done,

100

We'll turn with pleasure to a second one,
And give Valère, whose love has proven so true,
The wedded happiness which is his due.

NEW PLAYS

★ **THE EXONERATED by Jessica Blank and Erik Jensen.** Six interwoven stories paint a picture of an American criminal justice system gone horribly wrong and six brave souls who persevered to survive it. "The #1 play of the year...intense and deeply affecting..." –*NY Times*. "Riveting. Simple, honest storytelling that demands reflection." –*A.P.* "Artful and moving...pays tribute to the resilience of human hearts and minds." –*Variety*. "Stark...riveting...cunningly orchestrated." –*The New Yorker*. "Hard-hitting, powerful, and socially relevant." –*Hollywood Reporter*. [7M, 3W] ISBN: 0-8222-1946-8

★ **STRING FEVER by Jacquelyn Reingold.** Lily juggles the big issues: turning forty, artificial insemination and the elusive scientific Theory of Everything in this Off-Broadway comedy hit. "Applies the elusive rules of string theory to the conundrums of one woman's love life. Think *Sex and the City* meets *Copenhagen*." –*NY Times*. "A funny offbeat and touching look at relationships...an appealing romantic comedy populated by oddball characters." –*NY Daily News*. "Where kooky, zany, and madcap meet...whimsically winsome." –*NY Magazine*. "STRING FEVER will have audience members happily stringing along." –*TheaterMania.com*. "Reingold's language is surprising, inventive, and unique." –*nytheatre.com*. "...[a] whimsical comic voice." –*Time Out*. [3M, 3W (doubling)] ISBN: 0-8222-1952-2

★ **DEBBIE DOES DALLAS adapted by Erica Schmidt, composed by Andrew Sherman, conceived by Susan L. Schwartz.** A modern morality tale told as a comic musical of tragic proportions as the classic film is brought to the stage. "A scream! A saucy, tongue-in-cheek romp." –*The New Yorker*. "Hilarious! DEBBIE manages to have it all: beauty, brains and a great sense of humor!" –*Time Out*. "Shamelessly silly, shrewdly self-aware and proud of being naughty. Great fun!" –*NY Times*. "Racy and raucous, a lighthearted, fast-paced thoroughly engaging and hilarious send-up." –*NY Daily News*. [3M, 5W] ISBN: 0-8222-1955-7

★ **THE MYSTERY PLAYS by Roberto Aguirre-Sacasa.** Two interrelated one acts, loosely based on the tradition of the medieval mystery plays. "... stylish, spine-tingling...Mr. Aguirre-Sacasa uses standard tricks of horror stories, borrowing liberally from masters like Kafka, Lovecraft, Hitchock...But his mastery of the genre is his own...irresistible." –*NY Times*. "Undaunted by the special-effects limitations of theatre, playwright and *Marvel* comic-book writer Roberto Aguirre-Sacasa maps out some creepy twilight zones in THE MYSTERY PLAYS, an engaging, related pair of one acts...The theatre may rarely deliver shocks equivalent to, say, *Dawn of the Dead*, but Aguirre-Sacasa's work is fine compensation." –*Time Out*. [4M, 2W] ISBN: 0-8222-2038-5

★ **THE JOURNALS OF MIHAIL SEBASTIAN by David Auburn.** This epic one-man play spans eight tumultuous years and opens a uniquely personal window on the Romanian Holocaust and the Second World War. "Powerful." –*NY Times*. "[THE JOURNALS OF MIHAIL SEBASTIAN] allows us to glimpse the idiosyncratic effects of that awful history on one intelligent, pragmatic, recognizably real man..." –*NY Newsday*. [3M, 5W] ISBN: 0-8222-2006-7

★ **LIVING OUT by Lisa Loomer.** The story of the complicated relationship between a Salvadoran nanny and the Anglo lawyer she works for. "A stellar new play. Searingly funny." –*The New Yorker*. "Both generous and merciless, equally enjoyable and disturbing." –*NY Newsday*. "A bitingly funny new comedy. The plight of working mothers is explored from two pointedly contrasting perspectives in this sympathetic, sensitive new play." –*Variety*. [2M, 6W] ISBN: 0-8222-1994-8

DRAMATISTS PLAY SERVICE, INC.
440 Park Avenue South, New York, NY 10016 212-683-8960 Fax 212-213-1539
postmaster@dramatists.com www.dramatists.com

NEW PLAYS

★ **INTIMATE APPAREL by Lynn Nottage.** The moving and lyrical story of a turn-of-the-century black seamstress whose gifted hands and sewing machine are the tools she uses to fashion her dreams from the whole cloth of her life's experiences. "...Nottage's play has a delicacy and eloquence that seem absolutely right for the time she is depicting..." –*NY Daily News.* "...thoughtful, affecting...The play offers poignant commentary on an era when the cut and color of one's dress—and of course, skin—determined whom one could and could not marry, sleep with, even talk to in public." –*Variety.* [2M, 4W] ISBN: 0-8222-2009-1

★ **BROOKLYN BOY by Donald Margulies.** A witty and insightful look at what happens to a writer when his novel hits the bestseller list. "The characters are beautifully drawn, the dialogue sparkles..." –*nytheatre.com.* "Few playwrights have the mastery to smartly investigate so much through a laugh-out-loud comedy that combines the vintage subject matter of successful writer-returning-to-ethnic-roots with the familiar mid-life crisis." –*Show Business Weekly.* [4M, 3W] ISBN: 0-8222-2074-1

★ **CROWNS by Regina Taylor.** Hats become a springboard for an exploration of black history and identity in this celebratory musical play. "Taylor pulls off a Hat Trick: She scores thrice, turning CROWNS into an artful amalgamation of oral history, fashion show, and musical theater..." –*TheatreMania.com.* "...wholly theatrical...Ms. Taylor has created a show that seems to arise out of spontaneous combustion, as if a bevy of department-store customers simultaneously decided to stage a revival meeting in the changing room." –*NY Times.* [1M, 6W (2 musicians)] ISBN: 0-8222-1963-8

★ **EXITS AND ENTRANCES by Athol Fugard.** The story of a relationship between a young playwright on the threshold of his career and an aging actor who has reached the end of his. "[Fugard] can say more with a single line than most playwrights convey in an entire script...Paraphrasing the title, it's safe to say this drama, making its memorable entrance into our consciousness, is unlikely to exit as long as a theater exists for exceptional work." –*Variety.* "A thought-provoking, elegant and engrossing new play..." –*Hollywood Reporter.* [2M] ISBN: 0-8222-2041-5

★ **BUG by Tracy Letts.** A thriller featuring a pair of star-crossed lovers in an Oklahoma City motel facing a bug invasion, paranoia, conspiracy theories and twisted psychological motives. "...obscenely exciting...top-flight craftsmanship. Buckle up and brace yourself..." –*NY Times.* "...[a] thoroughly outrageous and thoroughly entertaining play...the possibility of enemies, real and imagined, to squash has never been more theatrical." –*A.P.* [3M, 2W] ISBN: 0-8222-2016-4

★ **THOM PAIN (BASED ON NOTHING) by Will Eno.** An ordinary man muses on childhood, yearning, disappointment and loss, as he draws the audience into his last-ditch plea for empathy and enlightenment. "It's one of those treasured nights in the theater—treasured nights anywhere, for that matter—that can leave you both breathless with exhilaration and...in a puddle of tears." –*NY Times.* "Eno's words...are familiar, but proffered in a way that is constantly contradictory to our expectations. Beckett is certainly among his literary ancestors." –*nytheatre.com.* [1M] ISBN: 0-8222-2076-8

★ **THE LONG CHRISTMAS RIDE HOME by Paula Vogel.** Past, present and future collide on a snowy Christmas Eve for a troubled family of five. "...[a] lovely and hauntingly original family drama...a work that breathes so much life into the theater." –*Time Out.* "...[a] delicate visual feast..." –*NY Times.* "...brutal and lovely...the overall effect is magical." –*NY Newsday.* [3M, 3W] ISBN: 0-8222-2003-2

DRAMATISTS PLAY SERVICE, INC.
440 Park Avenue South, New York, NY 10016 212-683-8960 Fax 212-213-1539
postmaster@dramatists.com www.dramatists.com

NEW PLAYS

★ **MATCH by Stephen Belber.** Mike and Lisa Davis interview a dancer and choreographer about his life, but it is soon evident that their agenda will either ruin or inspire them—and definitely change their lives forever. "Prolific laughs and ear-to-ear smiles." *–NY Magazine.* "Uproariously funny, deeply moving, enthralling theater. Stephen Belber's MATCH has great beauty and tenderness, and abounds in wit." *–NY Daily News.* "Three and a half out of four stars." *–USA Today.* "A theatrical steeplechase that leads straight from outrageous bitchery to unadorned, heartfelt emotion." *–Wall Street Journal.* [2M, 1W] ISBN: 0-8222-2020-2

★ **HANK WILLIAMS: LOST HIGHWAY by Randal Myler and Mark Harelik.** The story of the beloved and volatile country-music legend Hank Williams, featuring twenty-five of his most unforgettable songs. "[LOST HIGHWAY has] the exhilarating feeling of Williams on stage in a particular place on a particular night…serves up classic country with the edges raw and the energy hot…By the end of the play, you've traveled on a profound emotional journey: LOST HIGHWAY transports its audience and communicates the inspiring message of the beauty and richness of Williams' songs…forceful, clear-eyed, moving, impressive." *–Rolling Stone.* "…honors a very particular musical talent with care and energy… smart, sweet, poignant." *–NY Times.* [7M, 3W] ISBN: 0-8222-1985-9

★ **THE STORY by Tracey Scott Wilson.** An ambitious black newspaper reporter goes against her editor to investigate a murder and finds the *best* story…but at what cost? "A singular new voice…deeply emotional, deeply intellectual, and deeply musical…" *–The New Yorker.* "…a conscientious and absorbing new drama…" *–NY Times.* "…a riveting, tough-minded drama about race, reporting and the truth…" *–A.P.* "… a stylish, attention-holding script that ends on a chilling note that will leave viewers with much to talk about." *–Curtain Up.* [2M, 7W (doubling, flexible casting)] ISBN: 0-8222-1998-0

★ **OUR LADY OF 121st STREET by Stephen Adly Guirgis.** The body of Sister Rose, beloved Harlem nun, has been stolen, reuniting a group of life-challenged childhood friends who square off as they wait for her return. "A scorching and dark new comedy… Mr. Guirgis has one of the finest imaginations for dialogue to come along in years." *–NY Times.* "Stephen Guirgis may be the best playwright in America under forty." *–NY Magazine.* [8M, 4W] ISBN: 0-8222-1965-4

★ **HOLLYWOOD ARMS by Carrie Hamilton and Carol Burnett.** The coming-of-age story of a dreamer who manages to escape her bleak life and follow her romantic ambitions to stardom. Based on Carol Burnett's bestselling autobiography, *One More Time.* "…pure theatre and pure entertainment…" *–Talkin' Broadway.* "…a warm, fuzzy evening of theatre." *–BrodwayBeat.com.* "…chuckles and smiles of recognition or surprise flow naturally…a remarkable slice of life." *–TheatreScene.net.* [5M, 5W, 1 girl] ISBN: 0-8222-1959-X

★ **INVENTING VAN GOGH by Steven Dietz.** A haunting and hallucinatory drama about the making of art, the obsession to create and the fine line that separates truth from myth. "Like a van Gogh painting, Dietz's story is a gorgeous example of excess—one that remakes reality with broad, well-chosen brush strokes. At evening's end, we're left with the author's resounding opinions on art and artifice, and provoked by his constant query into which is greater: van Gogh's art or his violent myth." *–Phoenix New Times.* "Dietz's writing is never simple. It is always brilliant. Shaded, compressed, direct, lucid—he frames his subject with a remarkable understanding of painting as a physical experience." *–Tucson Citizen.* [4M, 1W] ISBN: 0-8222-1954-9

DRAMATISTS PLAY SERVICE, INC.
440 Park Avenue South, New York, NY 10016 212-683-8960 Fax 212-213-1539
postmaster@dramatists.com www.dramatists.com